AF265598

In This Flesh

DEATH AND THE WOMAN
Edvard Munch, 1894-1895

IN THIS FLESH

BY

KELLY LYNN CURRY

WESTMINSTER

ARCHIBALD CONSTABLE AND COMPANY

2 WHITEHALL GARDENS

1898

Also by Kelly Lynn Curry:

Breath and Bone

Those who know what it is like to experience constant pain yet keep going.

The Chronic Pain Warriors

Edvard Munch, 1895

WROTE THIS SOON AFTER MY FIRST BOOK WAS PUBLISHED.

THIS COLLECTION WAS WRITTEN WHILE DEALING WITH WEIGHTY MEDICAL DECISIONS AND ENDURING PAIN, BOTH PHYSICAL AND EMOTIONAL. I LEARNED SO MUCH THROUGH GRIEF AND SICKNESS. IT TAUGHT ME BOTH STRENGTH AND FRAGILITY CAN BE BEAUTIFUL.

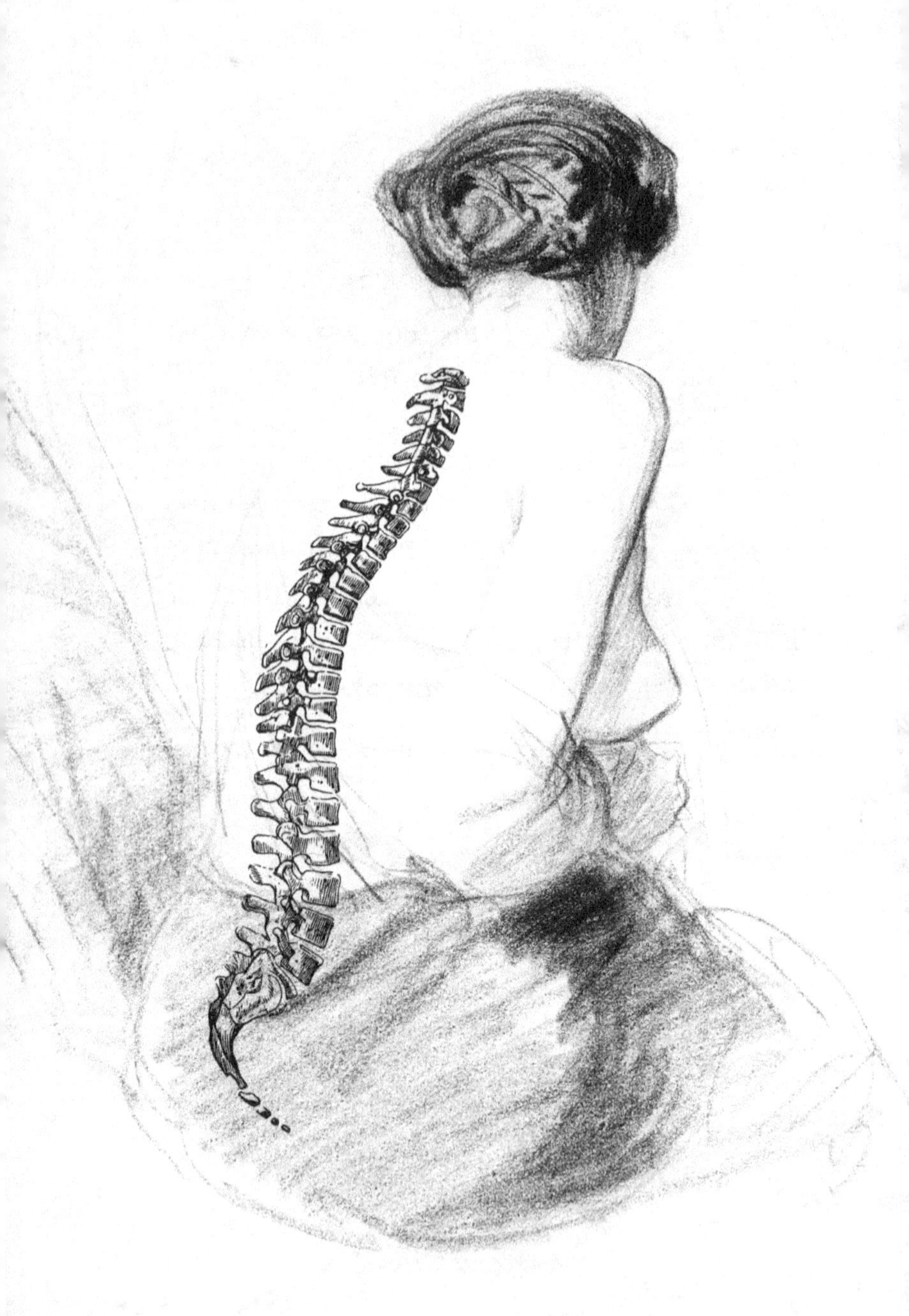

a poem starts
with a tingle
down the spine

IN THIS FLESH

I STAND BARE TO YOU

WITH ALL MY FOLLIES AND FLAWS

MY LOVE AND HEARTBREAK

EVERYTHING I AM AND COULD BE

DEFINED AND UNDEFINABLE

BREATHING THIS AIR OF POSSIBILITY

HOPING TO BE ANYTHING AT ALL

j'en aurait davantage que toutes mes
dernières.

J'espère Monsieur le Curé qu'à
présent mes lettres seront plus fréquentes
tque vous aurez plus souvent de mes
nouvelles.

Recevez Monsieur le Curé, avec
toute ma reconnaissance, les meilleurs
baisers de votre Augustin

Augustin Cornu
au 10ème d'infanterie 7e Compie
Auxonne (Côte d'Or)

Sigh into me
Ache in my bones
Crawl under my skin
Make a home in my soul

THE MEDULLA OBLONGATA (Figs. 415 and 416)

General Description.

The medulla oblongata, or *spinal bulb*, is the first division [of the brain, pro]ceeding from below upward. It has two extremities, superior [and inferior, and] four surfaces, dorsal, ventral, and two lateral. The inferior ex[tremity is] connected with the spinal cord; the upper has a similarly direc[ted one, connected with] the pons Varolii (Fig. 415). The surfaces in the upper half of [it are] distinct from each other; in the lower half each runs into the ot[her by insensible]

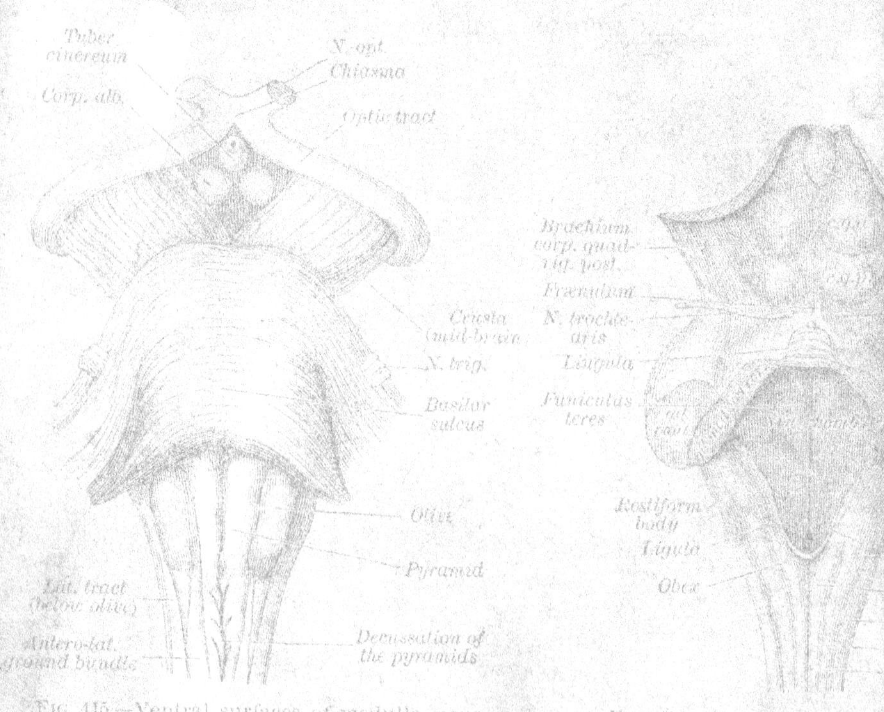

Fig. 415.—Ventral surfaces of medulla, pons, and mid-brain. (Gegenbaur.)

Fig. 416.—Dorsal surfaces of medulla, pons, and mid-brain. *c.q.a.* and *c.q.p.* corpora quadrigemina anterior and post. *ad pont.* = cut surface of peduncle of cerebellum. *ad med.* = cut surface of cerebellum. *ad cer.* = cut surface of superior peduncle. (Gegenbaur.)

gradations. Hence the outline of a cross-section of the upper half [would show] each of these surfaces distinctly, while a similar outline of the lo[wer half would] be almost that of a circle.

Scar tissue building up
A stitch in time, a stitch in skin
Scrapped knees and memories

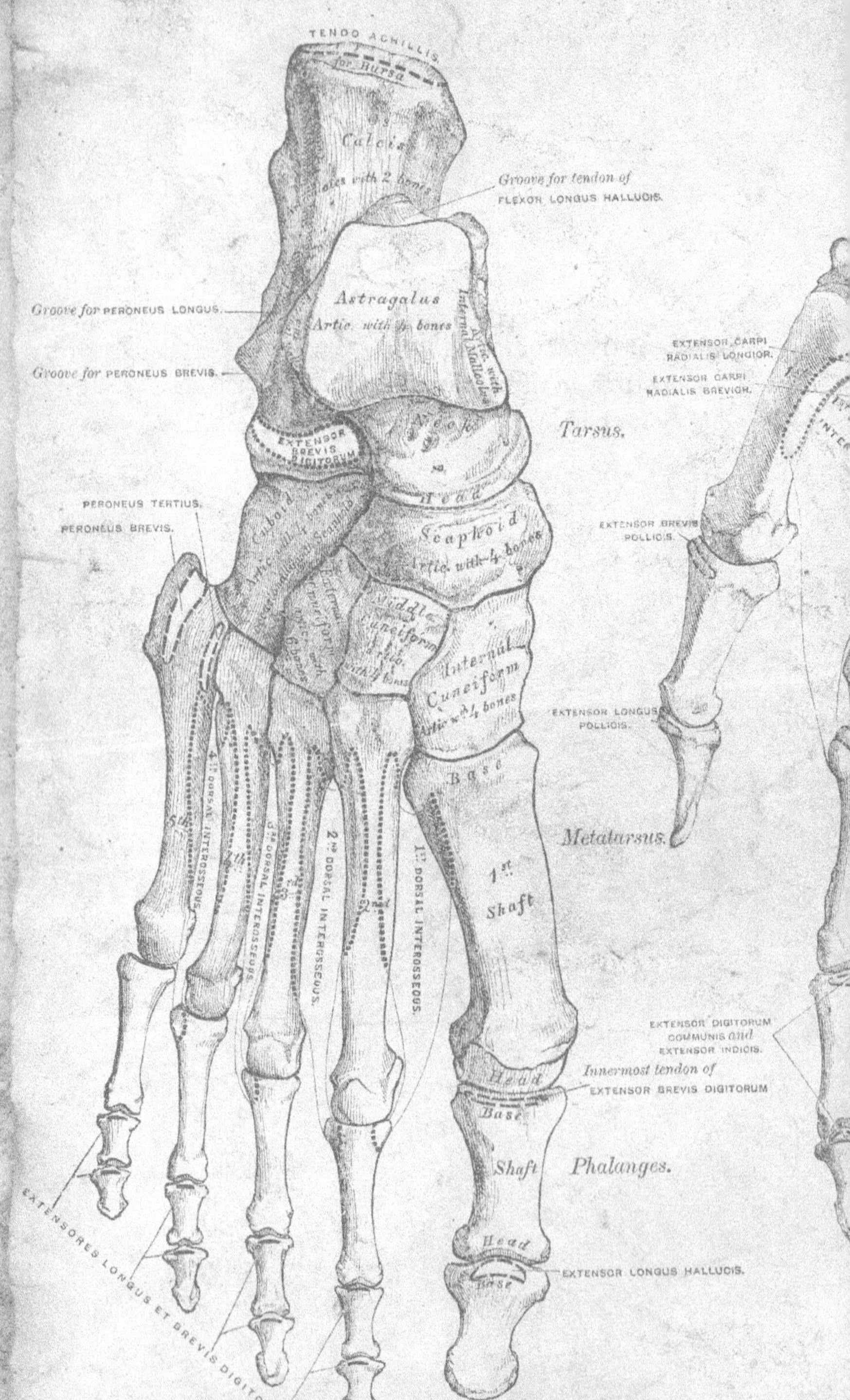

TENDO ACHILLIS.
for Bursa
Os Calcis
articulates with 2 bones
Groove for tendon of
FLEXOR LONGUS HALLUCIS.
Astragalus
Artic. with 5 bones
Artic. with Internal Malleolus
Groove for PERONEUS LONGUS.
Groove for PERONEUS BREVIS.
Neck
EXTENSOR BREVIS DIGITORUM
Head
Scaphoid
Artic. with 4 bones
Tarsus.
EXTENSOR CARPI RADIALIS LONGIOR.
EXTENSOR CARPI RADIALIS BREVIOR.
EXTENSOR BREVIS POLLICIS.
PERONEUS TERTIUS.
PERONEUS BREVIS.
Cuboid
Artic. with 4 bones
External Cuneiform
Middle Cuneiform
Internal Cuneiform
Artic. with 4 bones
Base
Metatarsus.
EXTENSOR LONGUS POLLICIS.
5th
4th DORSAL INTEROSSEOUS.
3rd DORSAL INTEROSSEOUS.
2nd DORSAL INTEROSSEOUS.
1st DORSAL INTEROSSEOUS.
1st Shaft
2nd
EXTENSOR DIGITORUM COMMUNIS and EXTENSOR INDICIS.
Innermost tendon of EXTENSOR BREVIS DIGITORUM
Head
Base
Shaft
Phalanges.
Head
Base
EXTENSOR LONGUS HALLUCIS.
EXTENSORES LONGUS ET BREVIS DIGITORUM

My Converse converse with the clouds
on at least a few occasions
I've met Phineas Fogg as he drifts past
and wave at Peter as he flies by that second star
But my shoelaces, they anchor me
Like Gulliver, they tie me down to earth

Bien cher M[...]

Je viens
de votre réponse
médicamenteux q[...]
avez envoyé
[...] vous
reçu le 10
Je vous envoie
[...]

There's a reason I am the way I am.
There's a story to your shadowed eyes and crooked grin.

Bloody from a battle I didn't wage
My arms laid down to rest
My sword never kissed red
My shield never took a blow
For all was done to me in words

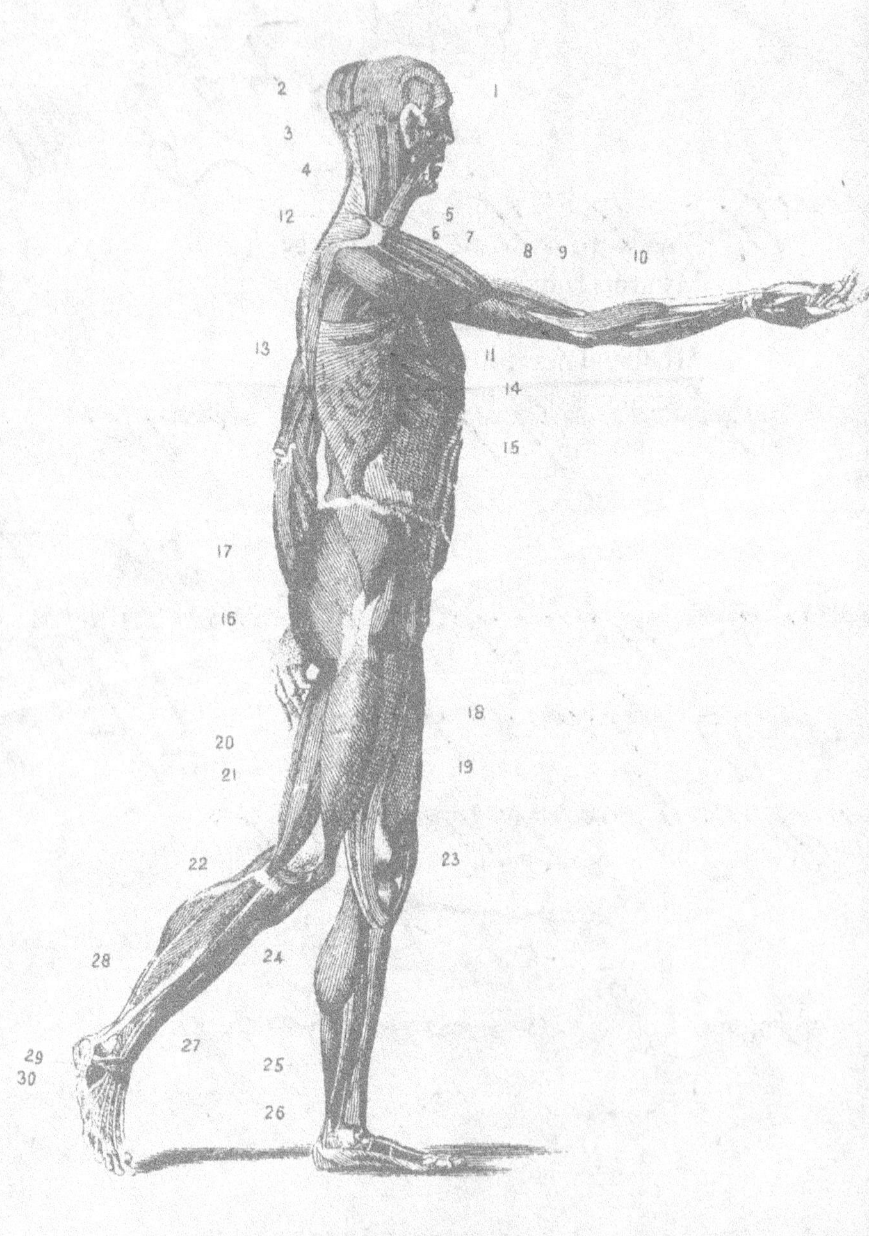

Fighting every day
Head versus heart
A boxing match
A duel?
Pistols at 10 paces
No seconds
Finger bent on the trigger
Aimed to kill

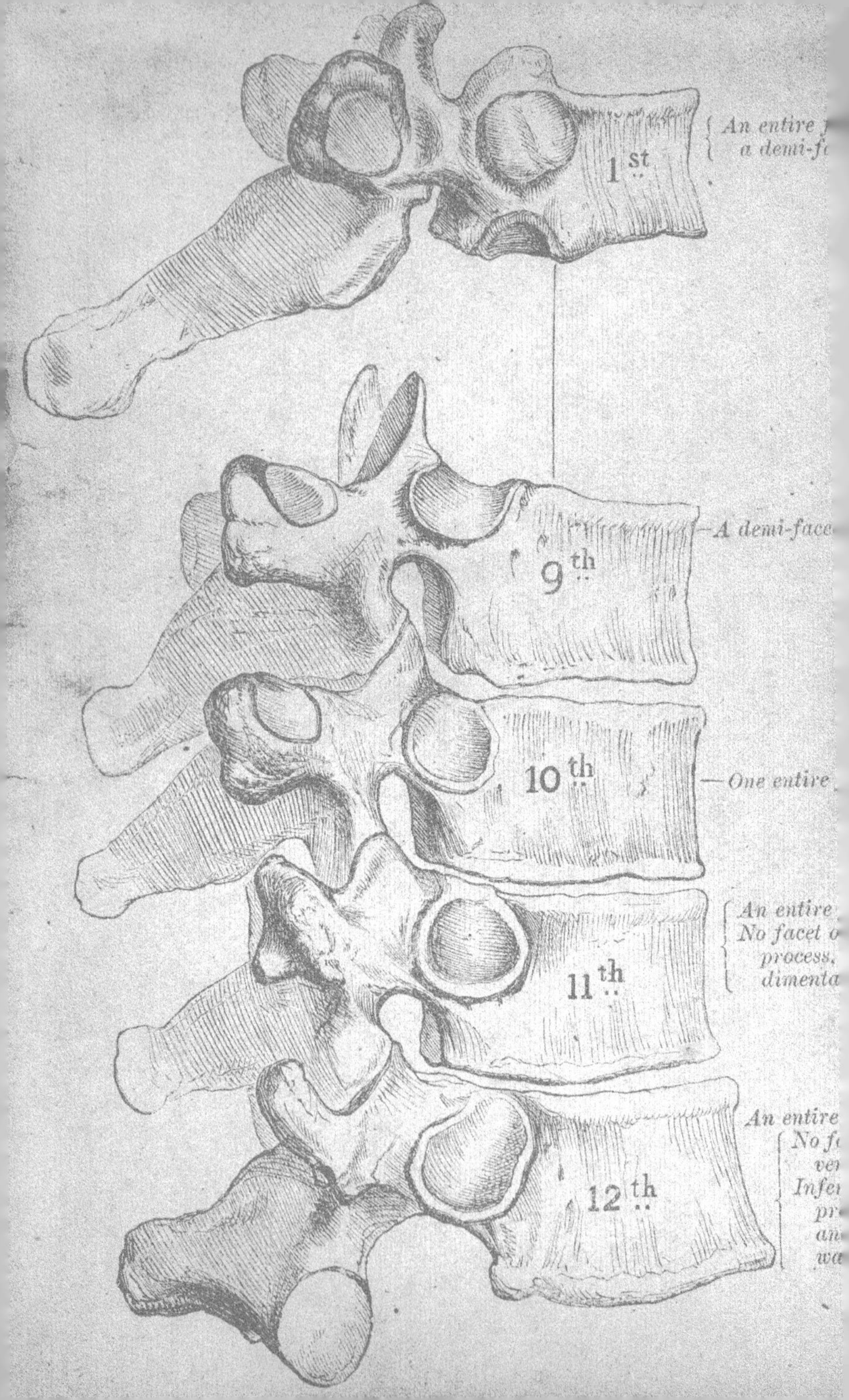

1st
{ An entire
a demi-fa
9th
- A demi-face
10th
- One entire
11th
{ An entire
No facet o
process,
dimenta
12th
An entire
{ No fo
ver
Infer
pr
an
wa

13

Crack. Snap. Splinter.
My body agonizes each sunrise
As I greet it timidly
Hoping that I don't awaken with fresh suffering

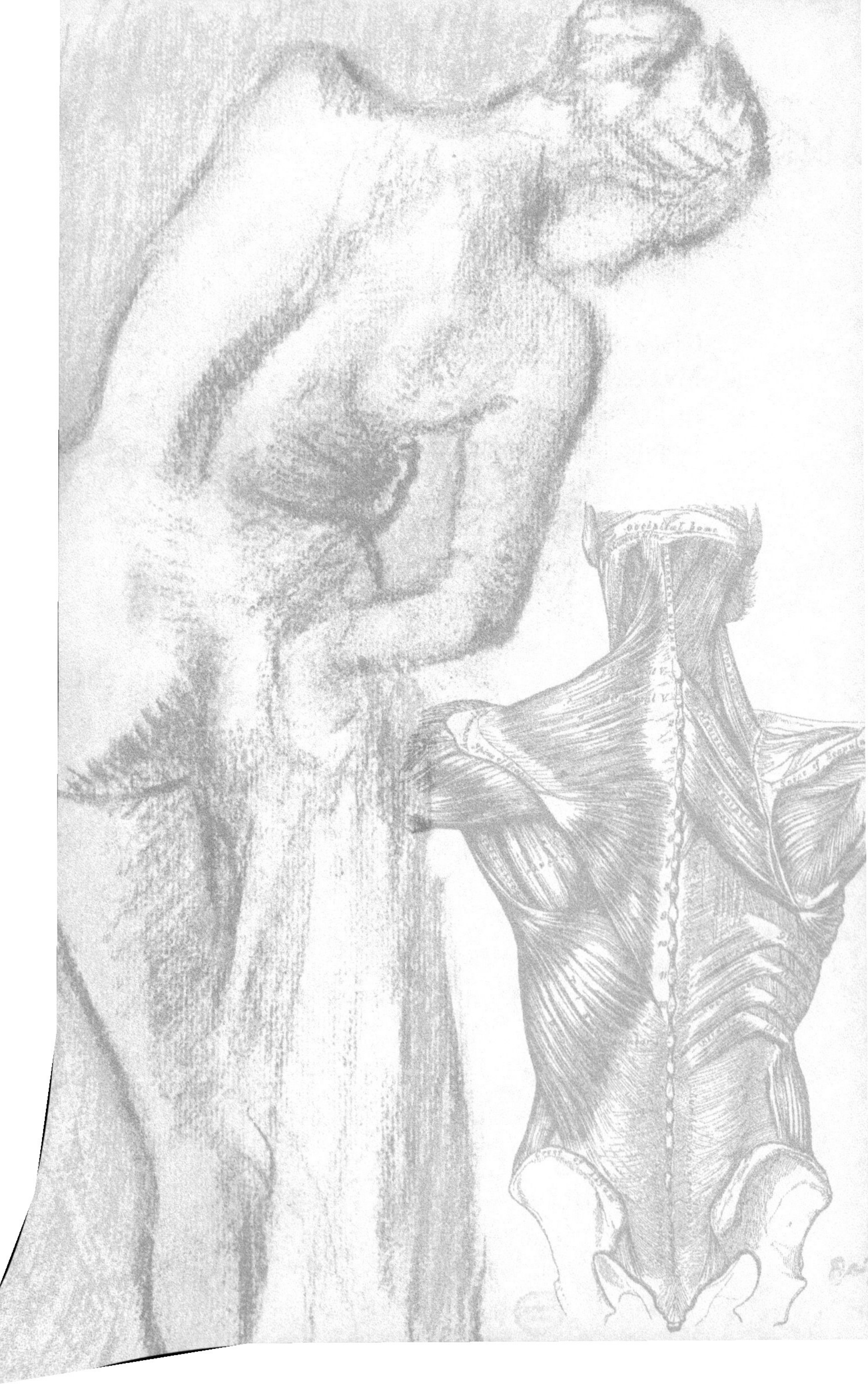
occipital bone

I am in the middle of
Love and Hate
With this body
I have been given.
She is here to help me
Yet denies me so much.
I fight the pain
And embrace the pleasure.
Hoping one day my body
Will be what it should.

Et dans tous les cas, je [...]
courants jour par jour —
Cambien je tiens par ma
cher beaucoup [...] Va[...]
Voyez vy persuadé — [...]
n'est-ce pas pour notre ch[...]
la volonté de dieu soit faite !
Votre tout dévoué
Aug. F[...]

Pills sliding down my throat
Don't let me choke
Side effects sober me
Drug me
Take me down the rabbit hole

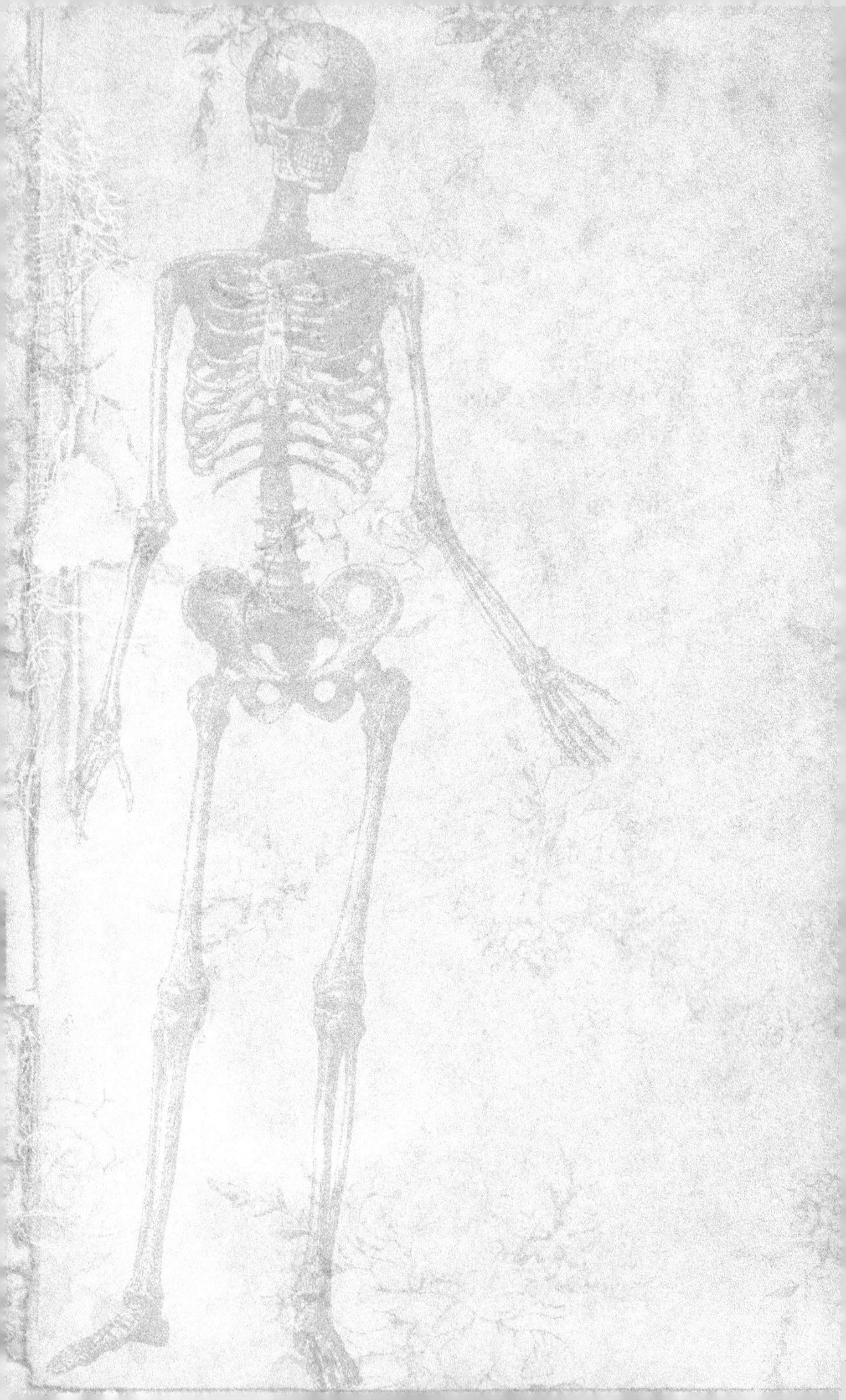

I miss my collarbones
I miss my dainty wrists
I miss my slender fingers
Now they are unrecognizable
All because of a pill
And its ravenous side effects

The **internal surface** (Fig. 155) is unequally divided into t
ntal projection of bone, the *palate process :* the portion abov

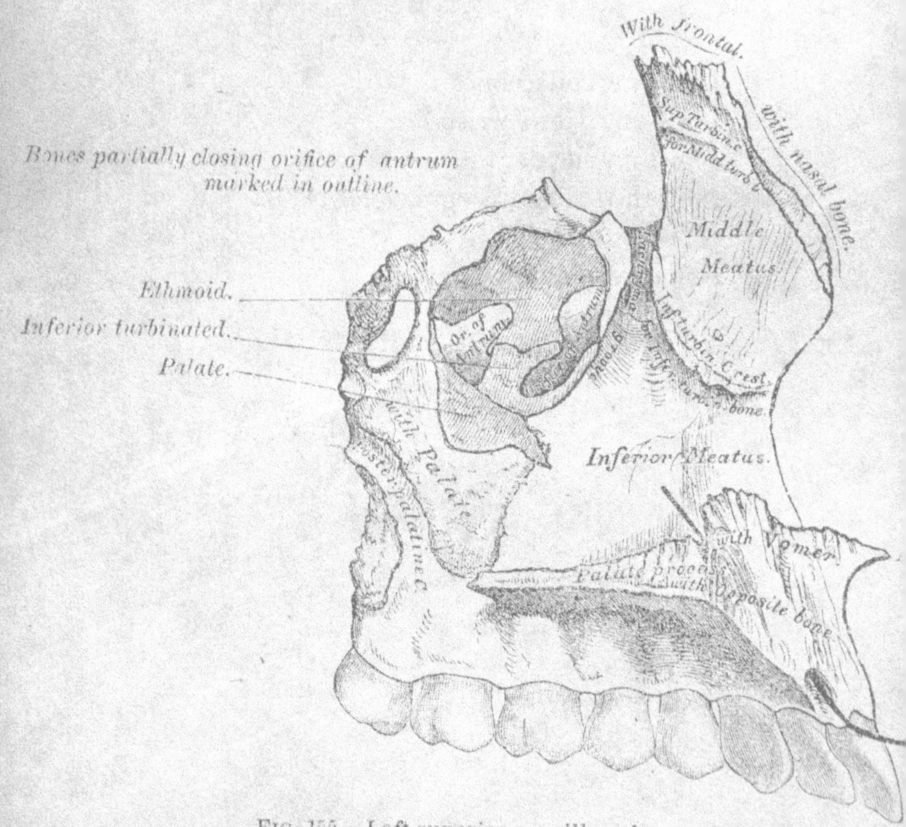

FIG. 155.—Left superior maxillary bone. Internal surface

ms part of the outer wall of the nasal fossæ; that below it
ity of the mouth.   The superior division of this surface prese
r opening leading into the *antrum of Highmore*.   At the up
rture are numerous broken cellular cavities, which in the art
sed in by the ethmoid and lachrymal bones   Below the ape

Pain is like robbery
It comes at night
In a dark alley
Cornering me at knifepoint
Stealing my sanity
My piece of mind
this is a stick up
An assault on my senses

Groove for superior longitudinal sinus.
Grooves for anterior meningeal artery.
Foramen cæcum.
Crista galli.
Slit for nasal nerve.
Groove for nasal nerve.
Anterior ethmoidal foramen.
Orifices for olfactory nerves.
Posterior ethmoidal foramen.
Ethmoidal spine.

Olfactory grooves.

Optic foramen.
Optic groove.
Olivary process.
Anterior clinoid process.
Middle clinoid process.

Posterior clinoid process.

Groove for 6th nerve.
Foramen lacerum medium.
Orifice of carotid canal.
Depression for Gasserian ganglion.

Meatus auditorius internus.
Slit for dura mater.
Superior petrosal groove.
Foramen lacerum posterius.
Anterior condyloid foramen.
Aqueductus vestibuli.
Posterior condyloid foramen.

Foramen magnum.

Mastoid foramen.

Posterior meningeal grooves.

Anterior Fossa.
Orbital Plate of Frontal.
Body & Lesser Wing of Sphenoid.
Gt'd Wing.
Middle Fossa.
Petrous Portion of Temporal.
Posterior Fossa.
Occipital.
Gr. for Lateral Sinus.

FIG. 172.—Base of the skull. Inner or cerebral surface.

They say monsters only live in the dark,
then why are these creatures gnawing at the walls
at daybreak,
at noon,
until I can't fight it anymore.
With heavy lids,
I battle with nothing more than my mind.
No sword or shield.
No army of men.
I fight with only the willpower to meet Dawn
 as she stretches and brings the sun,
her fiery red fingertips grasping at the embers of morning.

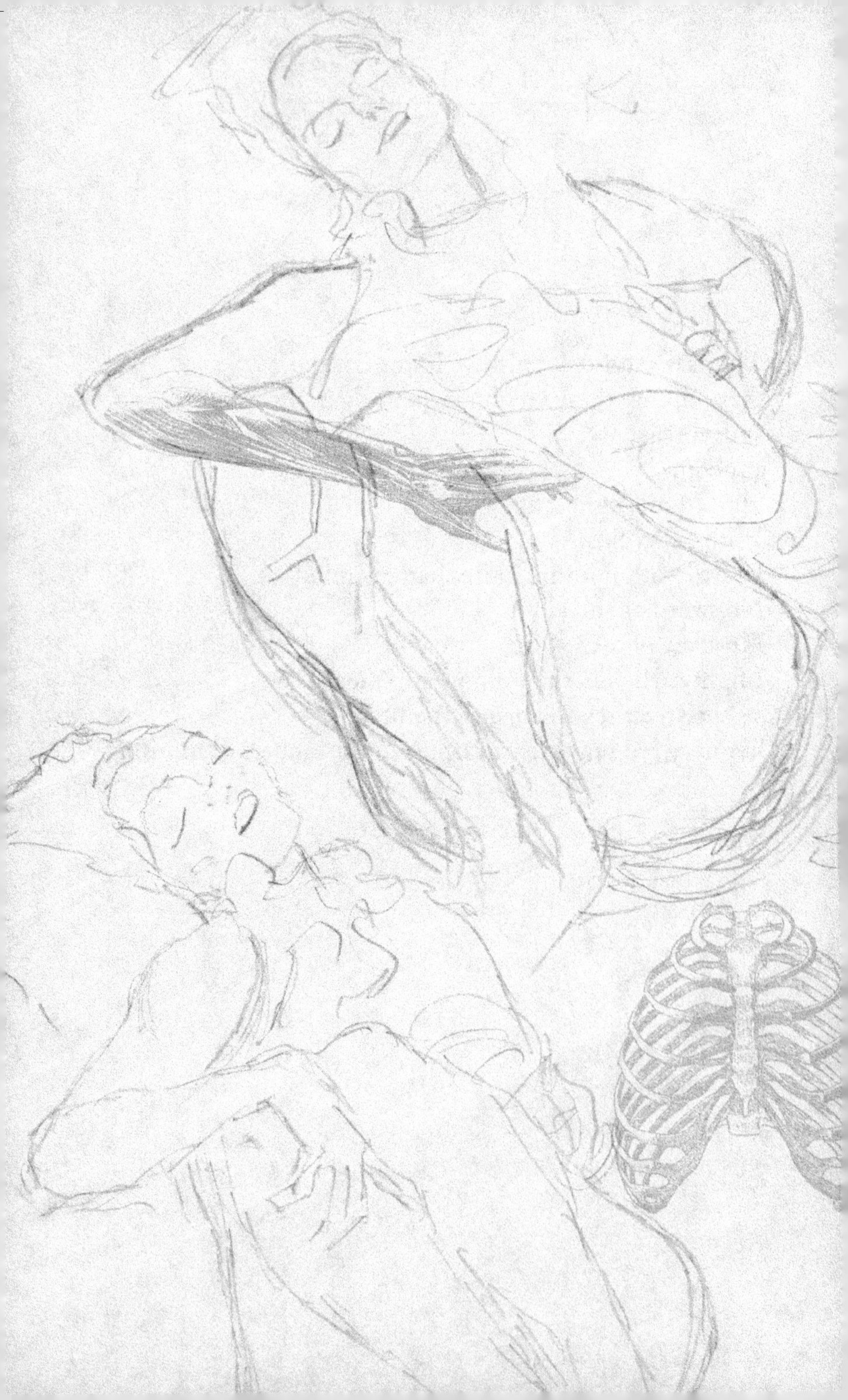

I want my old body back
Before the medication ravaged it
And distorted it
Gave it side effects
And turned it into this wreckage

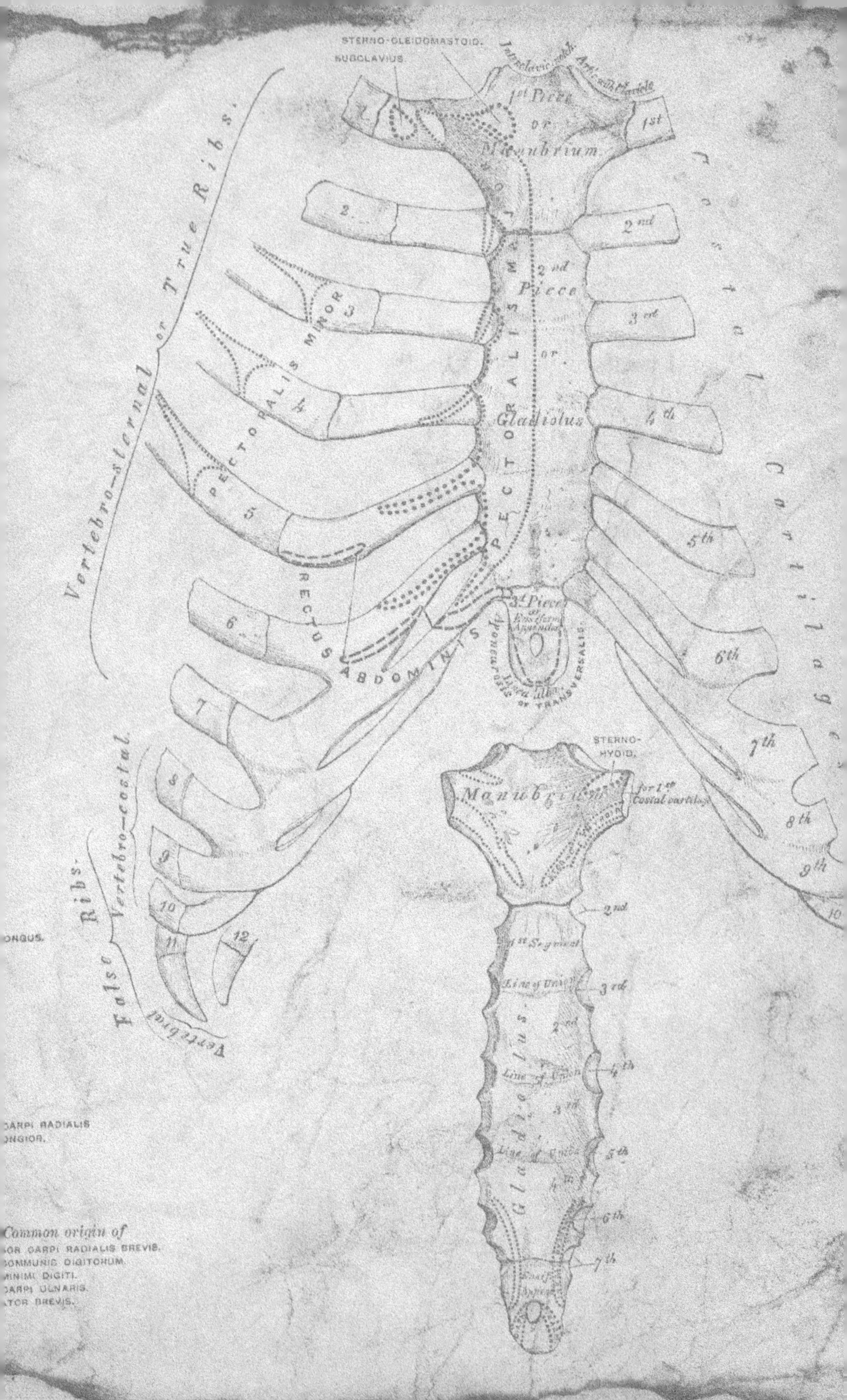

STERNO-CLEIDOMASTOID.
SUBCLAVIUS.
Interclavicular Artic. with Clavicle
1st Piece
or
Manubrium
1st
2nd
2nd
Piece
3rd
or
Gladiolus
4th
Vertebro-sternal or True Ribs.
PECTORALIS MINOR
PECTORALIS
3
4
5
RECTUS ABDOMINIS
5th
6
6th
3d Piece or Ensiform Appendix
Aponeurosis with Ilia or TRANSVERSALIS
7
7th
False Ribs.
Vertebro-costal.
8
STERNO-HYOID.
Manubrium
for 1st Costal cartilage
9
8th
10
9th
11
12
10
Vertebral
2nd
1st Segment
Line of Union
3rd
2nd
Line of Union
4th
Gladiolus
3rd
Line of Union
5th
4th
6th
CARPI RADIALIS
LONGIOR.
7th
Common origin of
OR CARPI RADIALIS BREVIS.
COMMUNIS DIGITORUM.
MINIMI DIGITI.
CARPI ULNARIS.
TOR BREVIS.
ONGUS.

27

A paradox of pain
Clinical, dialed in
Linoleum: too cold against bare feet
The air is stale and warm,
Letting the smells of vomit and medicine linger
This hospital room is all too familiar

Luscanne le 31 octobre 1907.

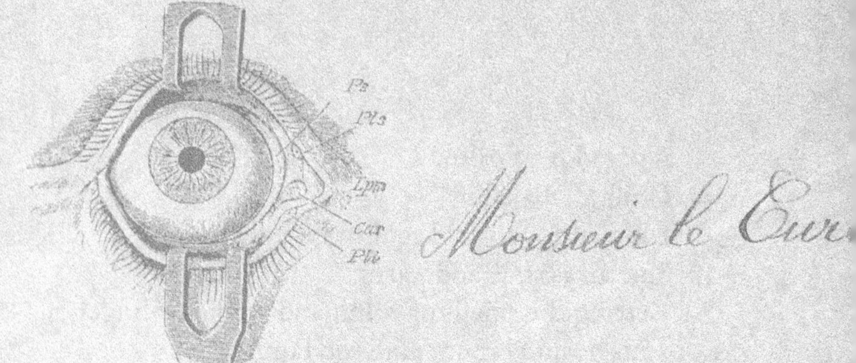

Monsieur le Curé

C'est vraiment honteux de ma part de ne pas vous avoir née de mes nouvelles, mais croyez bien Monsieur le Curé que ce n'est pas de ma faute, car depuis ma rentrée à la caserne, je n'ai pas une minute à moi; ce soir qu bonne partie de mes camarades sortie je   , et par con quent un peu de repos pour nous, j'en profite pour vous en ner.

Enveloped in vulnerability
Wide-eyed and bushy-browed

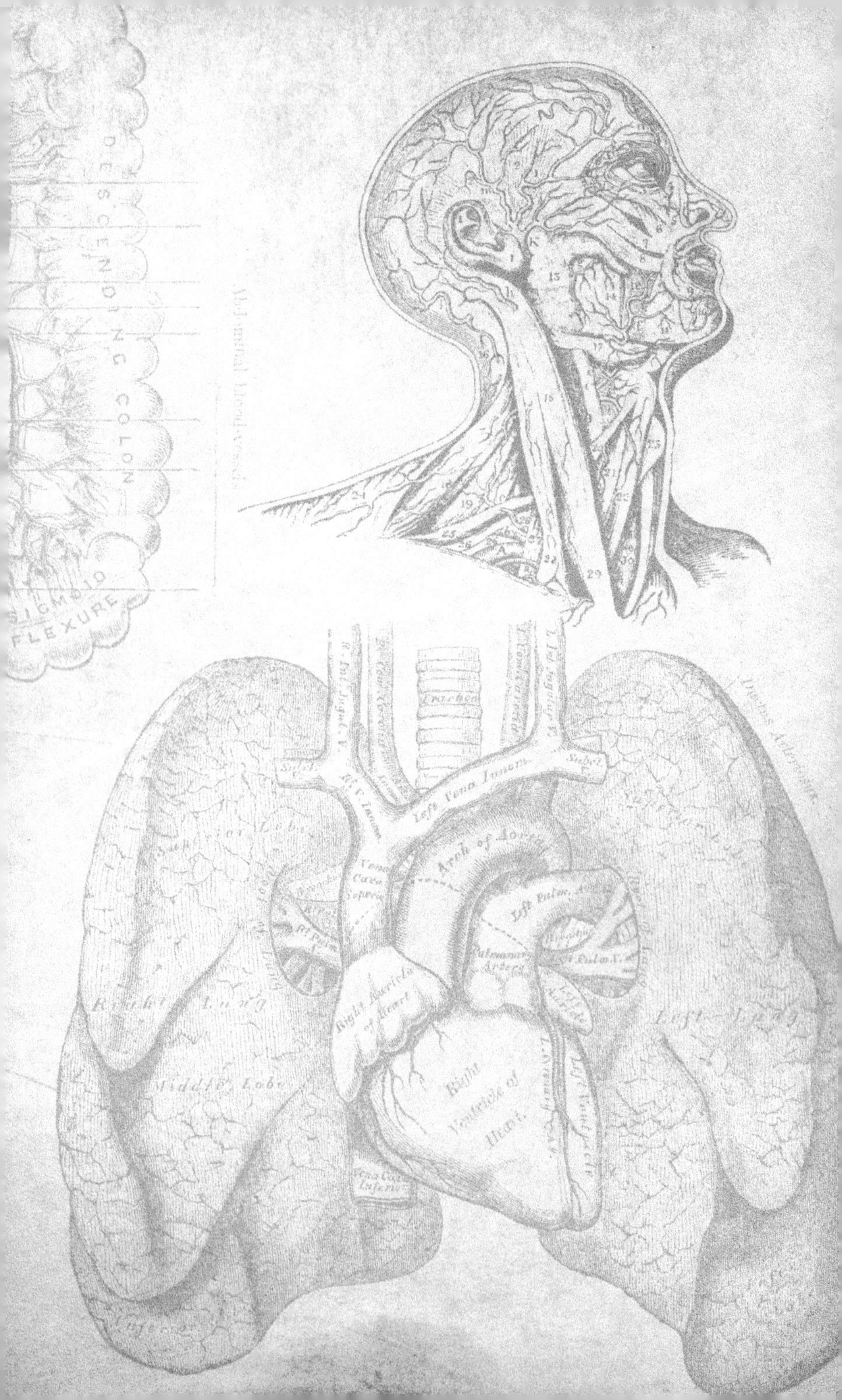

DESCENDING COLON
SIGMOID FLEXURE
Abdominal blood-vessels
Trachea
Arch of Aorta
Left Vena Innom.
Vena Cava Superior
Pulmonary Artery
Left Pulm. A.
Left Pulm. V.
Right Auricle of Heart
Right Ventricle of Heart
Right Lung
Middle Lobe
Left Lung
Vena Cava Inferior

Fleeting energy
Drowning in sleep
Barely enough to keep my head above the fray
Lungs filling with water
Sinking, slowly down down down
Reaching for the surface as exhaustion creeps in

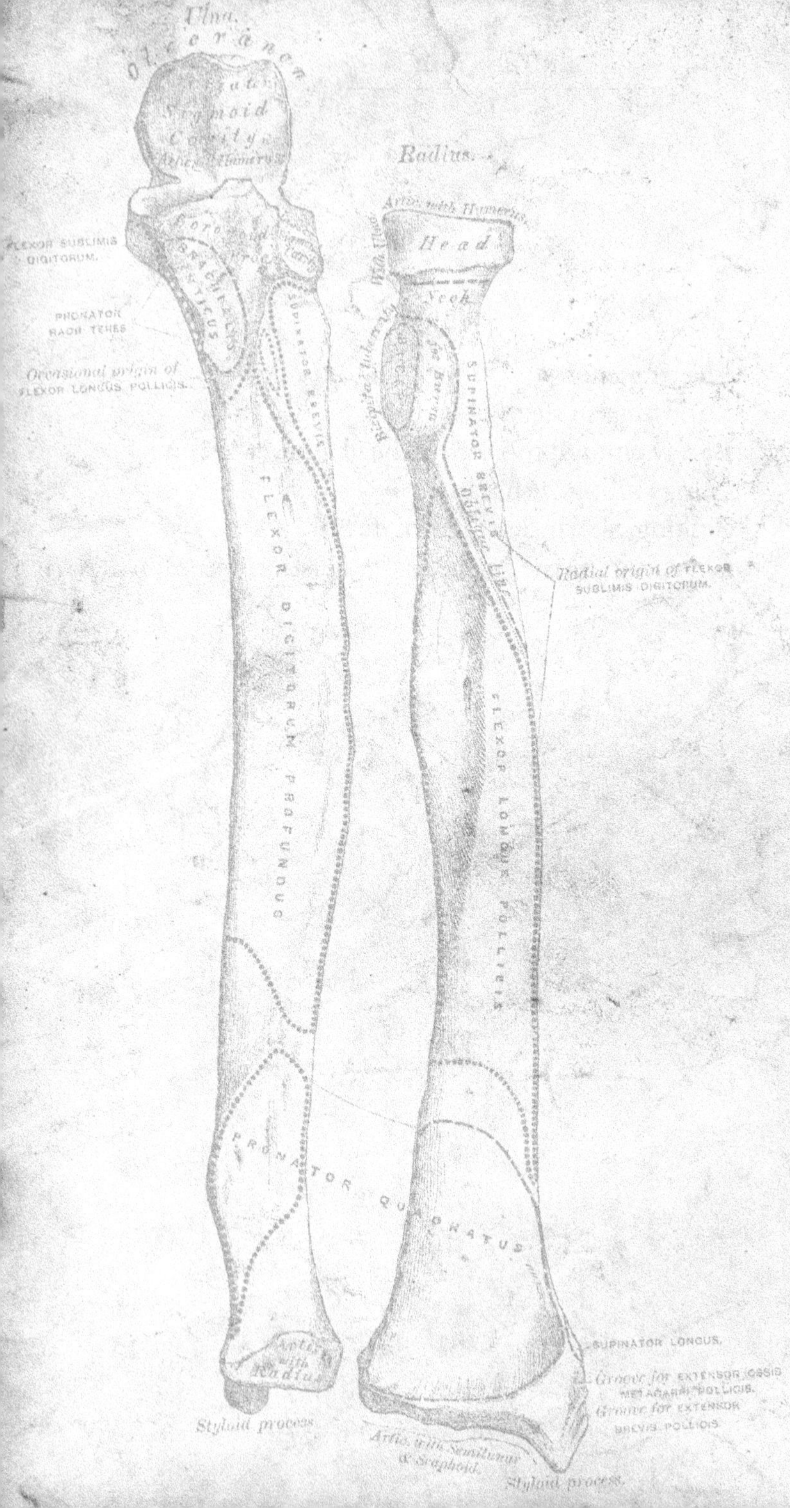

Ulna.
Olecranon
Greater Sigmoid Cavity
Artic. w. Humerus
Radius.
Artic. with Humerus
Head
Neck
FLEXOR SUBLIMIS DIGITORUM.
PRONATOR RADII TERES
Coronoid Process
BRACHIALIS ANTICUS
Lesser Sigmoid Cavity
SUPINATOR BREVIS
Occasional origin of FLEXOR LONGUS POLLICIS.
Bicipital Tuberosity
for Biceps
SUPINATOR BREVIS
Oblique Line
FLEXOR DIGITORUM PROFUNDUS
Radial origin of FLEXOR SUBLIMIS DIGITORUM.
FLEXOR LONGUS POLLICIS
PRONATOR QUADRATUS
Artic. with Radius
Styloid process
SUPINATOR LONGUS.
Groove for EXTENSOR OSSIS METACARPI POLLICIS.
Groove for EXTENSOR BREVIS POLLICIS.
Artic. with Semilunar & Scaphoid.
Styloid process.

I am a prisoner to this bracelet fastened around my wrist.
Blood pressure cuffs and IVs ordained like jewelry
My energy and morale falter
Pharmaceuticals flow through my recovering veins
The cheery nurse's bedside manner is anything but infectious
I can't wait to leave this place.

The neurons of my body
are being twisted apart slowly yet swiftly.
Each one teasing me, agitating my soul.
Hyperactive.
Energy flowing through my bloodstream erratically.
Bouncing off my insides like an adult in a bouncy castle:
Destroying it with each jump.

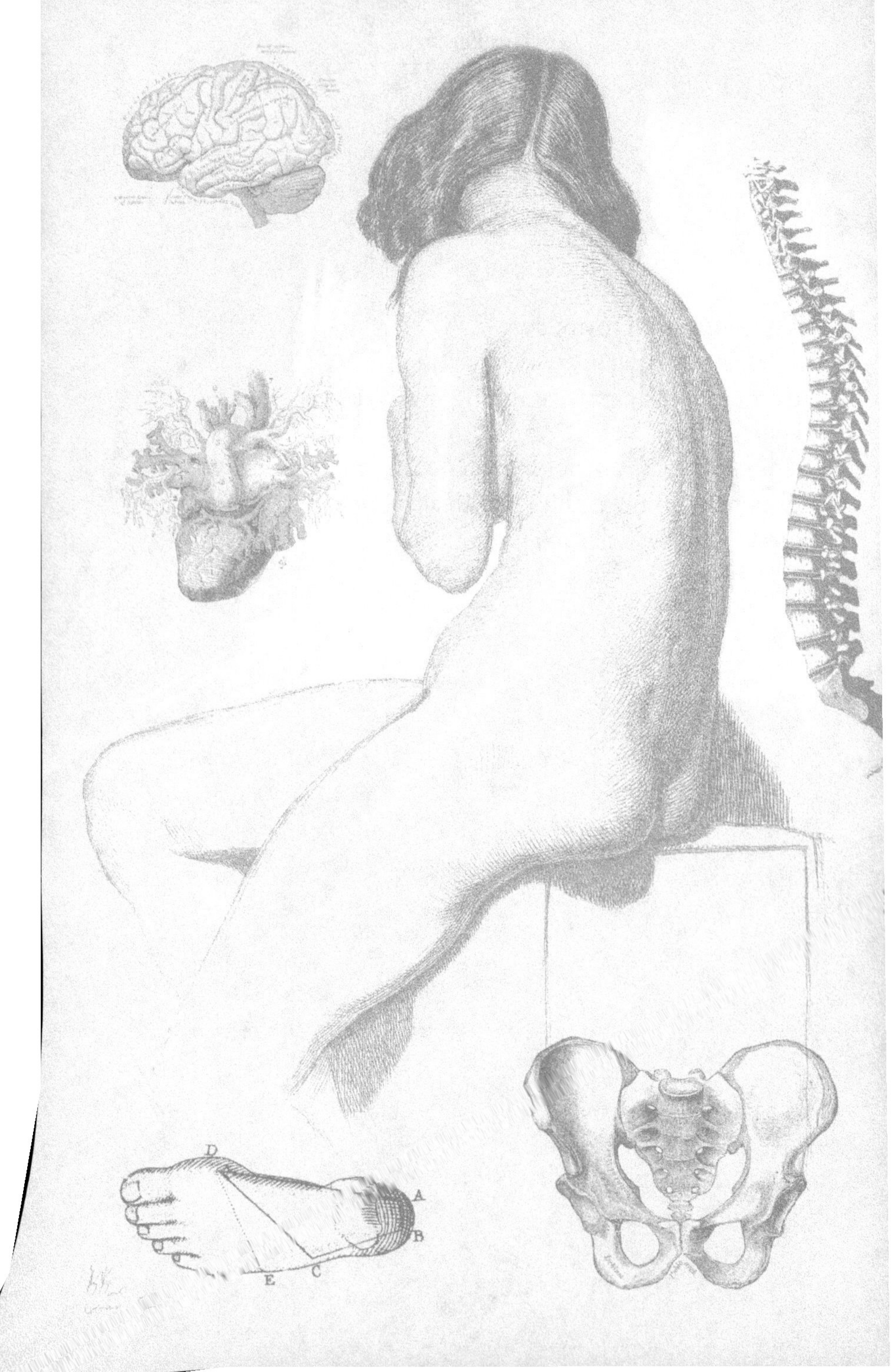
D
A
B
E
C

Betrayal
Abandoned by the vessel
Rejected
Homeless inside four walls of flesh

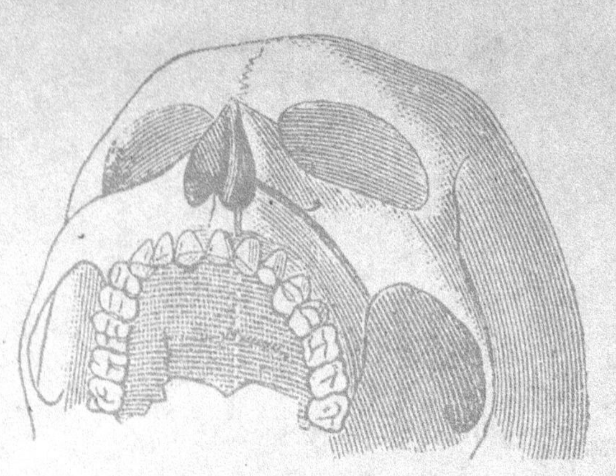

Corrugator supercilii is a small, narrow, pyramidal muscle, placed
tremity of the eyebrow, be-
he Occipito-frontalis and
ris palpebrarum muscles.
from the inner extremity
superciliary ridge; from
its fibres pass upward and
to be inserted into the
rface of the orbicularis, op-
e middle of the orbital arch.
ions.—By its *anterior sur-*
the Occipito-frontalis and
ris palpebrarum muscles;
posterior surface, with the
bone and supratrochlear

Levator palpebræ will be
l with the muscles of the
egion.

Tensor tarsi (Horner's
(Fig. 270) is a small thin
bout three lines in breadth
in length, situated at the
de of the orbit, behind the
uli. It arises from the crest
cent part of the orbital sur-
e lachrymal bone, and, pass-

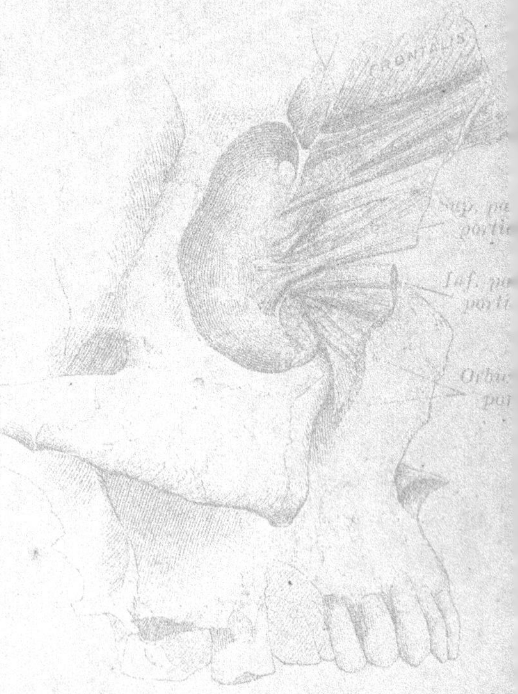

Fig. 270.—Inner part of orbicularis palpebrarum from behind. (Henle.)

ss the lachrymal sac, divides into two slips, which cover the lachr
nd are inserted into the tarsal plates internal to the puncta lachryn
s appear to be continuous with those of the palpebral portion o
ris palpebrarum; it is occasionally very indistinct.

Static breathing
Wistful thinking
Heartbeat racing
Morphine dripping
Fighting the heaviness
That is tangled with my blood

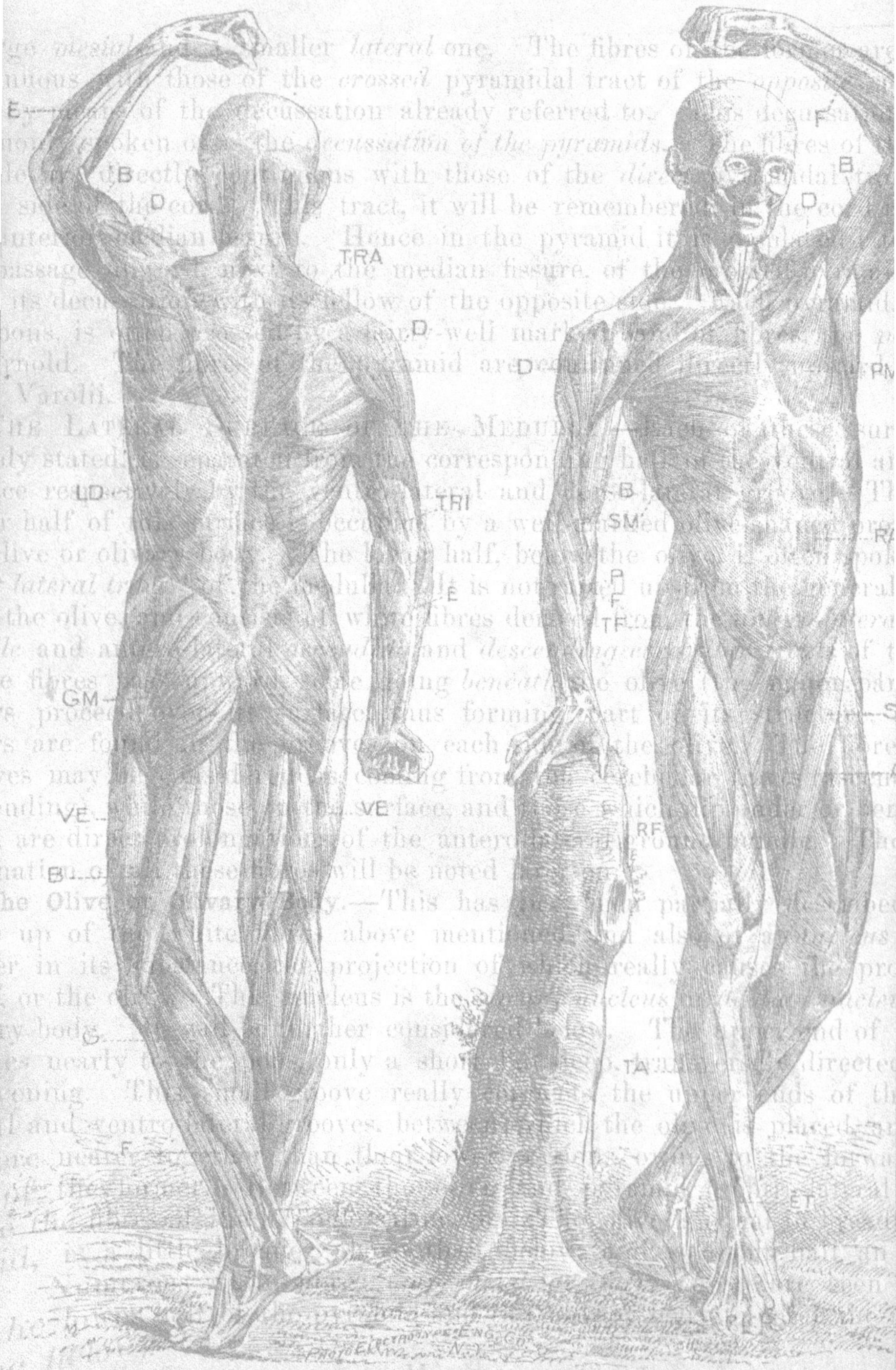

We sit here
comparing wounds
"Mine is deeper"
Bleeding gaping flesh

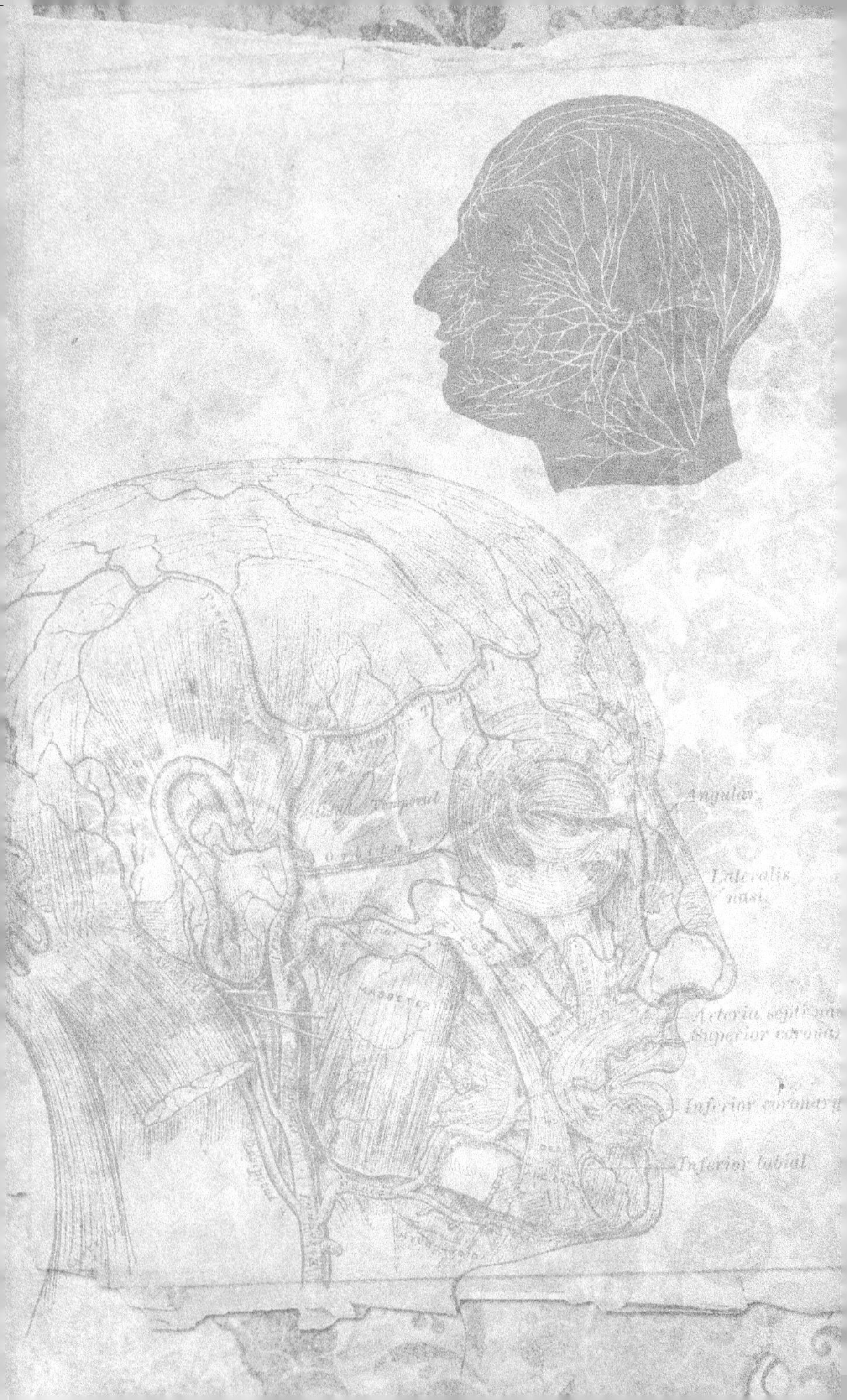

Angular
Lateralis nasi
Arteria septi
Superior coronary
Inferior coronary
Inferior labial

the caffeine and romance are coursing through my veins wildly.

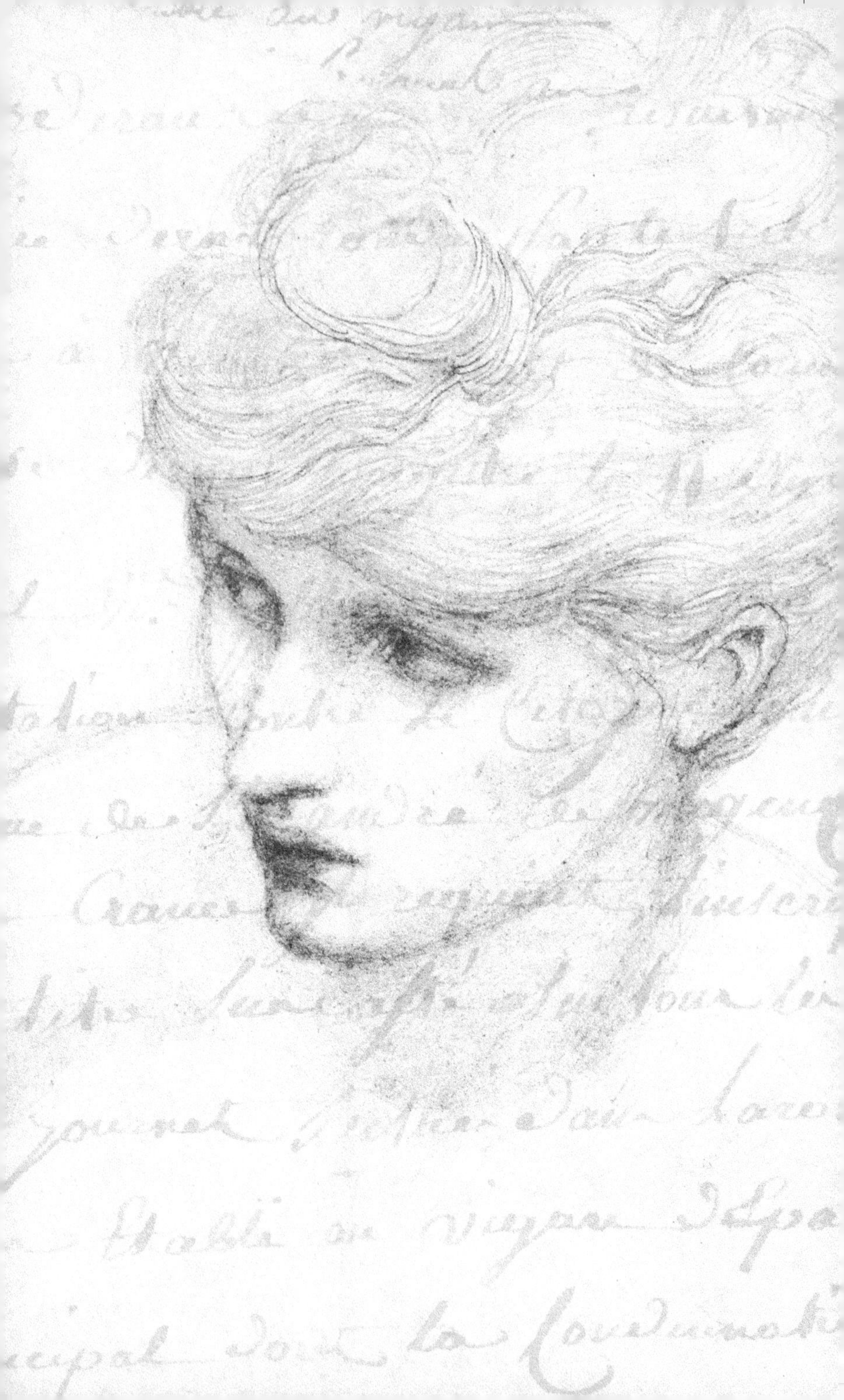

There's a storm in my stomach
Every time you brush against my blizzard skin
There's lightning in my veins
Every time you kiss my hurricane lips.

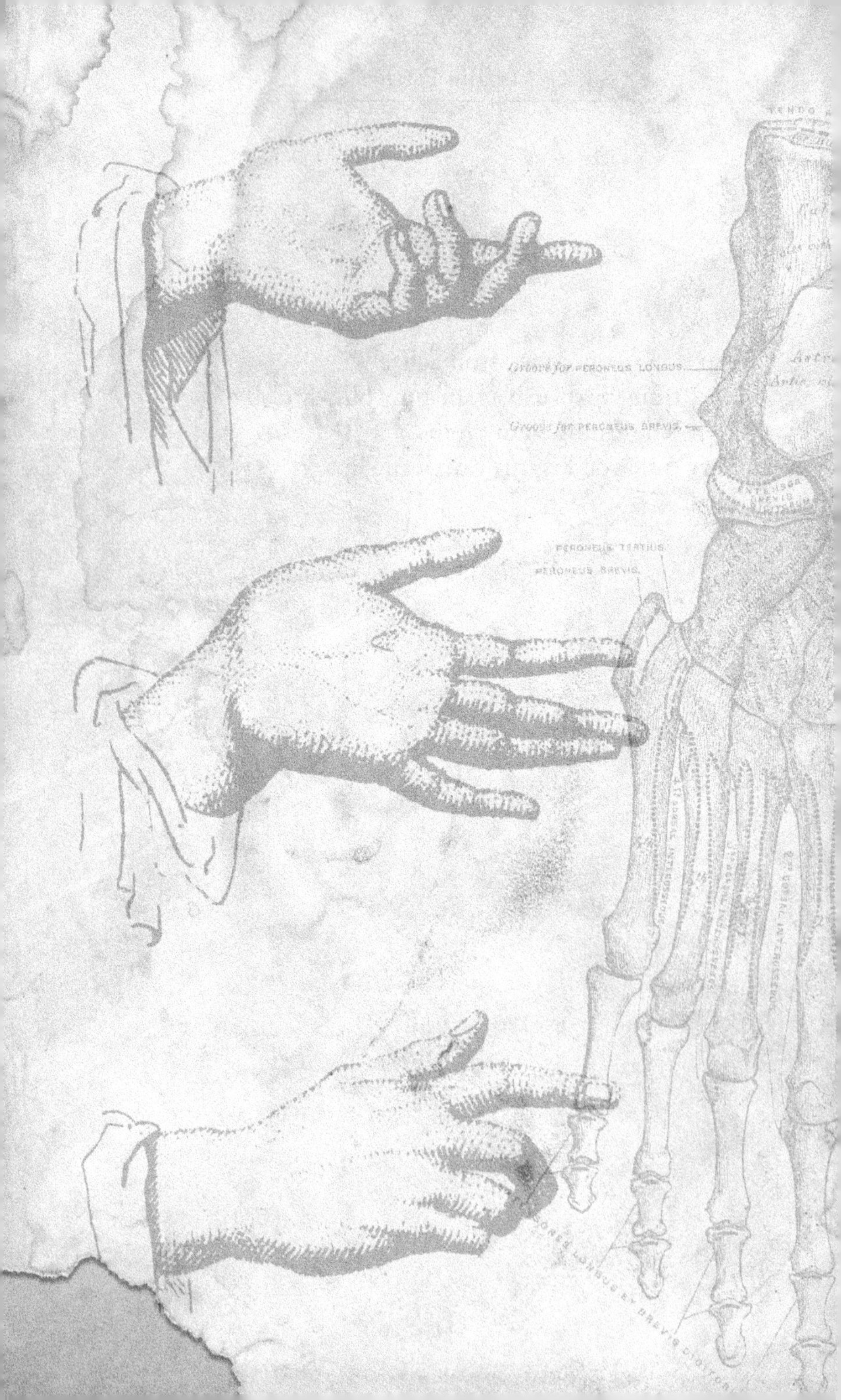

Groove for PERONEUS LONGUS
Groove for PERONEUS BREVIS
PERONEUS TERTIUS
PERONEUS BREVIS

I place you down on a bed of my bones
I lay lilies by your breast
Your porcelain skin glistens in the moonlit snow
With only my soul to keep you warm

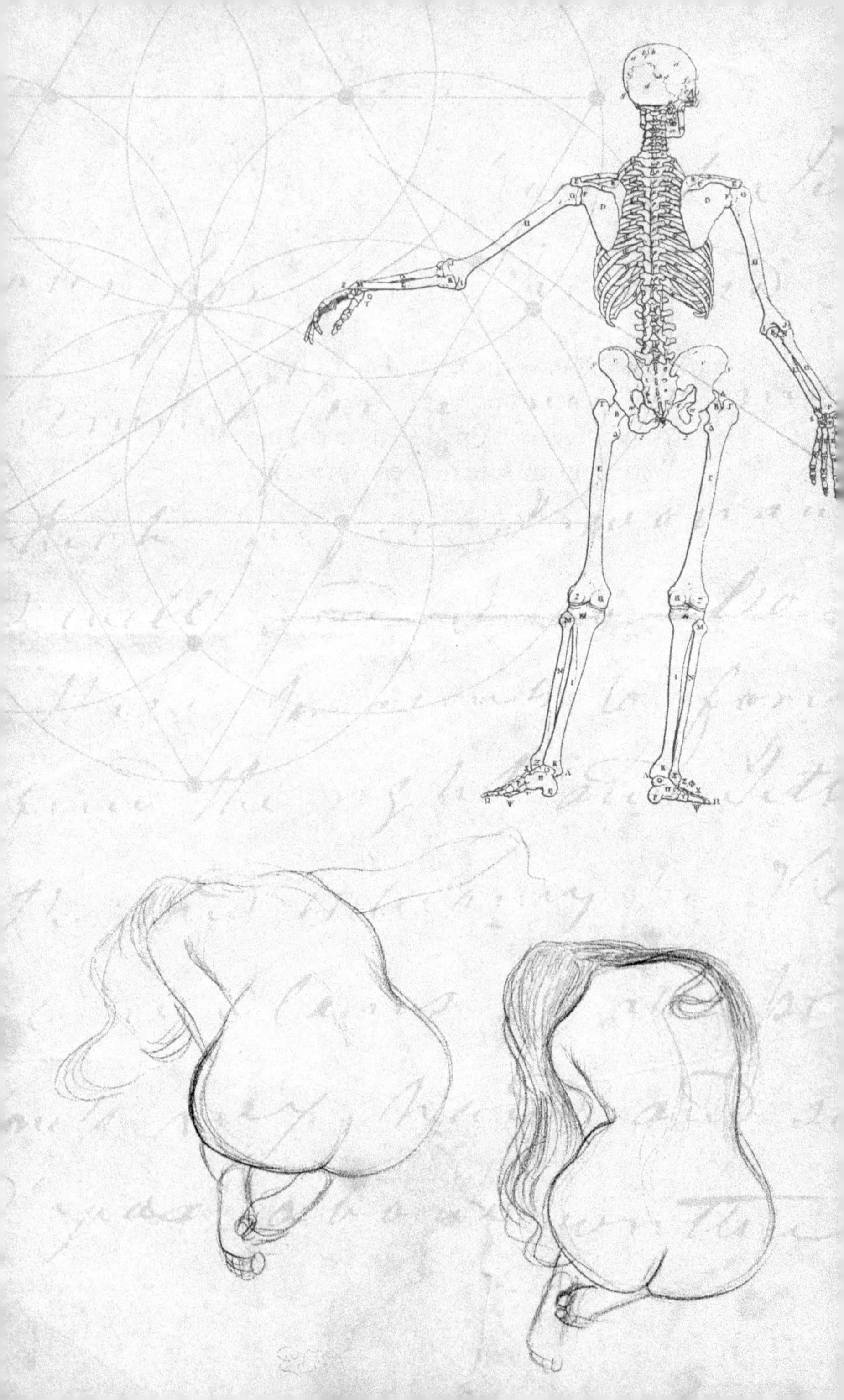

You toyed with me like a marionette
Made me dance
Then cut my strings
Dropped me on the floor
To collect dust forevermore

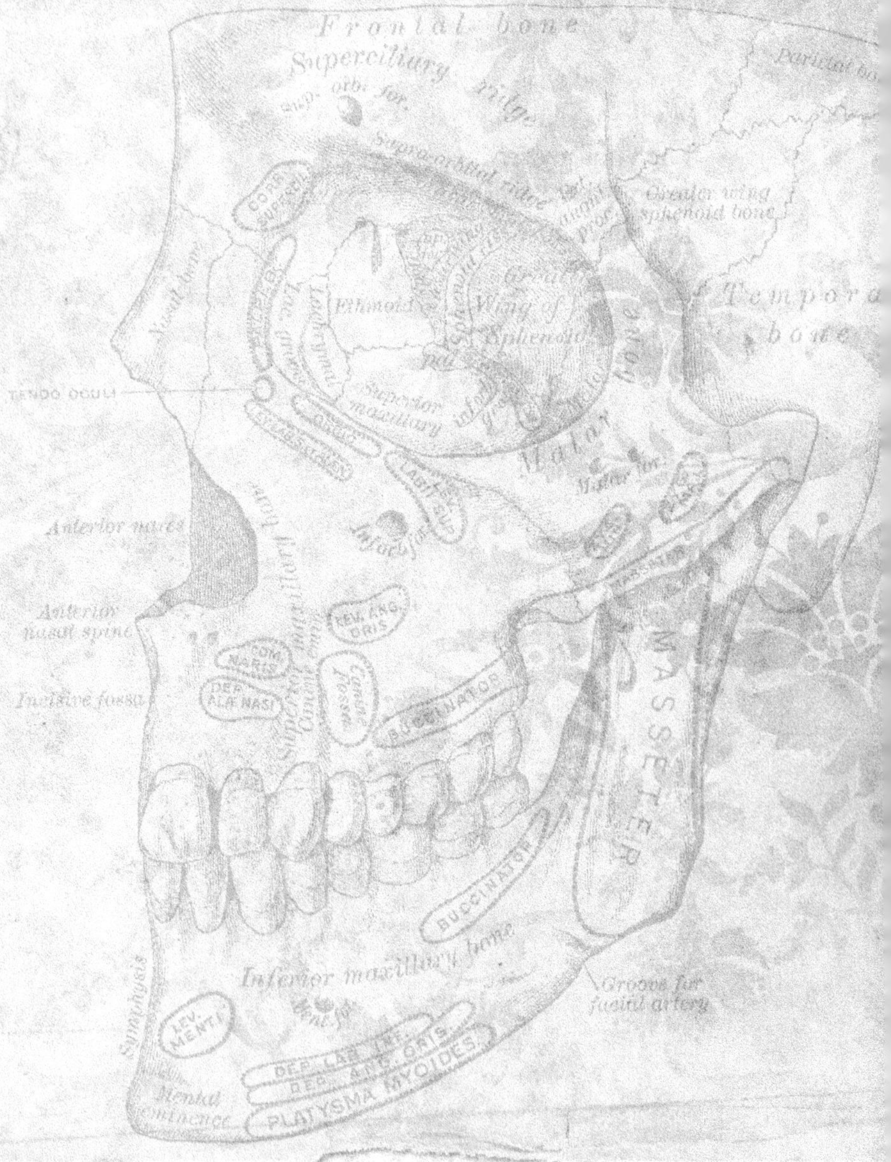

Frontal bone
Superciliary ridge
sup. orb. for.
Supra-orbital ridge
Parietal bone
Greater wing sphenoid bone
Temporal bone
Nasal bone
Ethmoid
Lachrymal
Greater Wing of Sphenoid
Superior maxillary
Malar bone
Malar for.
TENDO OCULI
Anterior nares
Anterior nasal spine
Incisive fossa
COM. NARIS
DEP. ALA NASI
LEV. ANG. ORIS
BUCCINATOR
MASSETER
BUCCINATOR
Symphysis
LEV. MENTI
Mental eminence
Inferior maxillary bone
Groove for facial artery
DEP. LAB. INF.
DEP. ANG. ORIS
PLATYSMA MYOIDES

It's been too long since I've heard your voice
Melodic, gruff, soothing,
Sing me to sleep with your soft words
Kiss my senses with your sweet sounds
Drift away on your ambiance

The Alumnae [illegible] it

year to receive into their

that [illegible]

[illegible]

[illegible]

[illegible]

[illegible]

[illegible]

Class of 22 [illegible] give

hearty welcome.

You'd sink an armada with those lips.

Frontal Lobe.

E.

Sup. Frontal Lobe

Mid. Frontal Lobe

Inf. Frontal Lobe

Præcentral Fissure

Ascending Frontal Lobe

Fissure of Rolando

Ascending Parietal Lobe

Post Central Fiss.

Intra Par.

Sup. Marginal C.

Horizontal Fiss. of Sylvius

Sup. Temp. Sphen. Conv.

Sup. Temp. Sphen. Fiss.

Mid. Temp. Sphen. Con.

Inf. Temp. Sphen. F.

Inf. Temp. Sphen.

ascending fissure of Sylvius.

Fissure of Sylvius.

Temporo-sphenoidal. Lobe.

No jury, no judge
You executed me.
Swift.
The Guillotine snapped
You did not allow a second to
Give me piece of mind.

72 — Parti avec ________

4 Sursol nel de 3895 Delmas
Riaud net de 500. ________

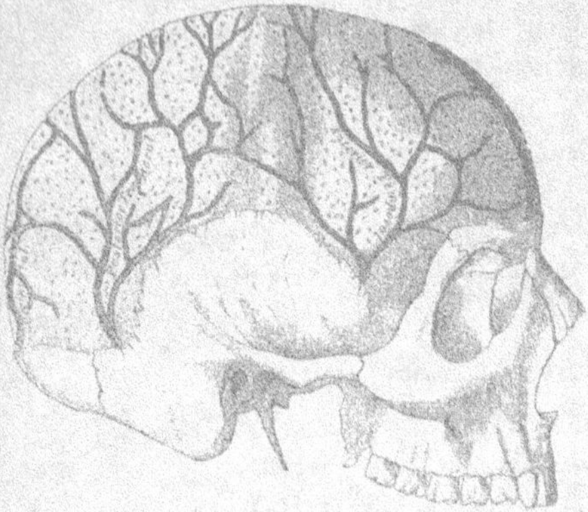

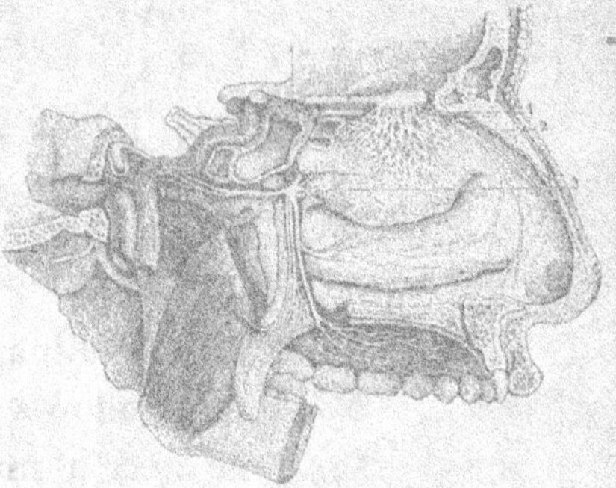

Rembourse à Sursol menus frais
Delmas nel de sa valeur
val. Riaud et Terunel ________
à Chauvel remult de 3000 ________

à à ceux de Garcin ________

96. 00

71. 50

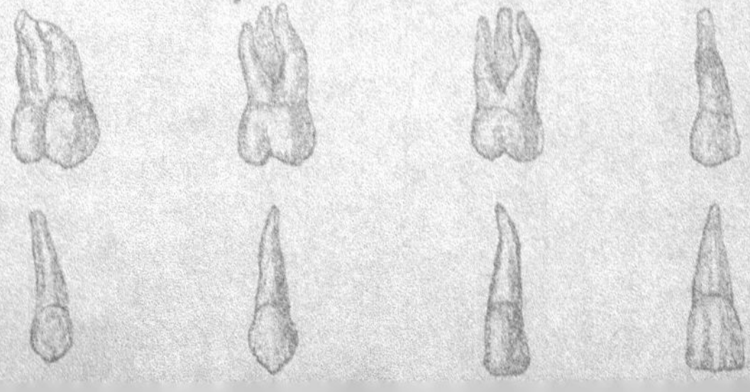

Your words - clever
Like venom when you are with your friends
They bite, but I fight back

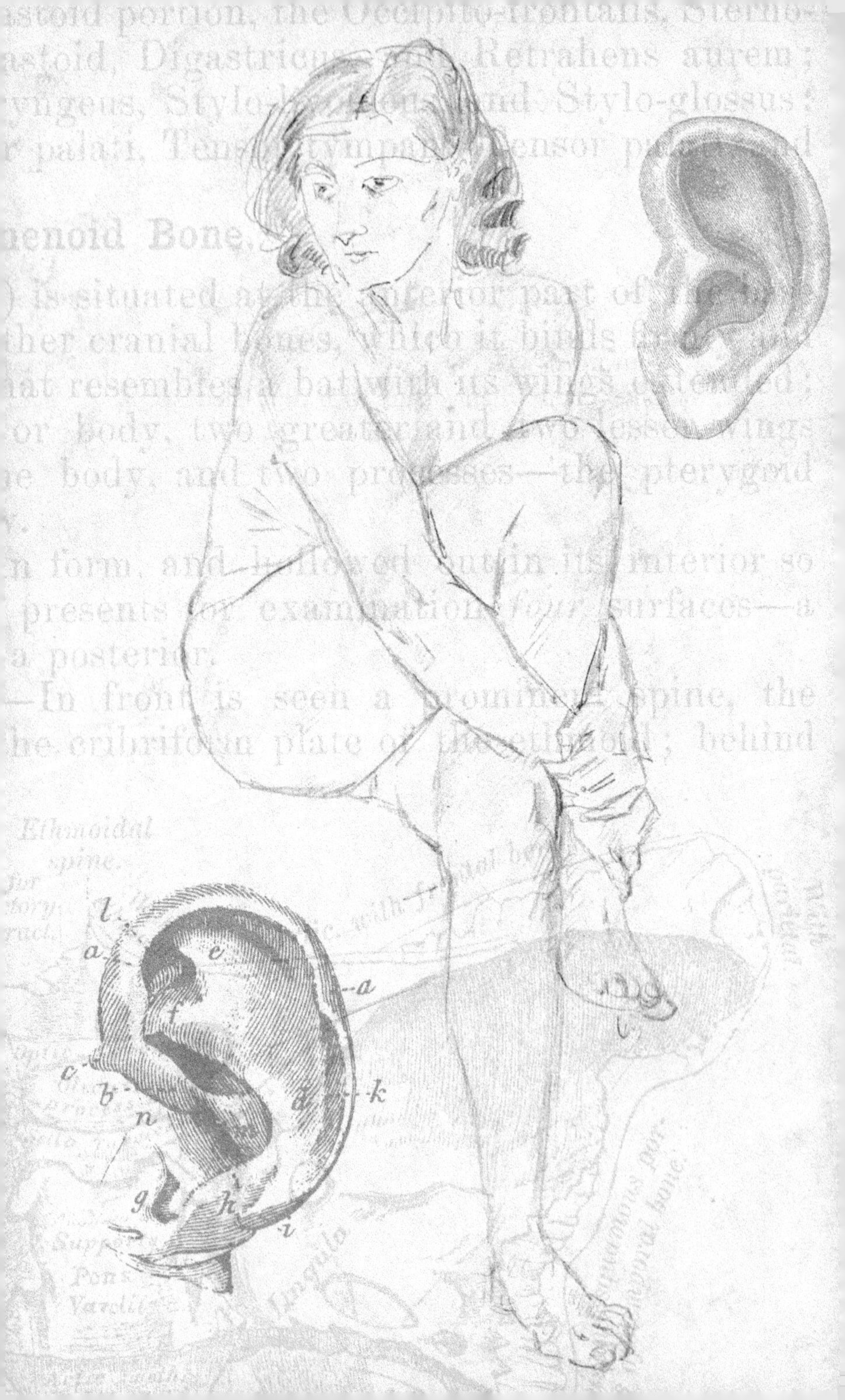

astoid portion, the Occipito-frontalis, Sterno-
astoid, Digastricus, and Retrahens aurem;
yngeus, Stylo-... and Stylo-glossus;
palati, Tensor tympani, ... tensor pa... and

enoid Bone,

) is situated at the anterior part of the
ther cranial bones, which it binds ...
at resembles a bat with its wings extended;
or body, two greater and two lesser wings
e body, and two processes—the pterygoid

n form, and hollowed out in its interior so
presents for examination *four* surfaces—a
a posterior.
—In front is seen a prominent spine, the
he cribriform plate of the ethmoid; behind

Ship in a bottle
I've never launched to sea
But I've been lured to the rocks
Tether me to the ship, to the bow
Like a figurehead
'cause I hear music that has come
from the sweet lips of sirens

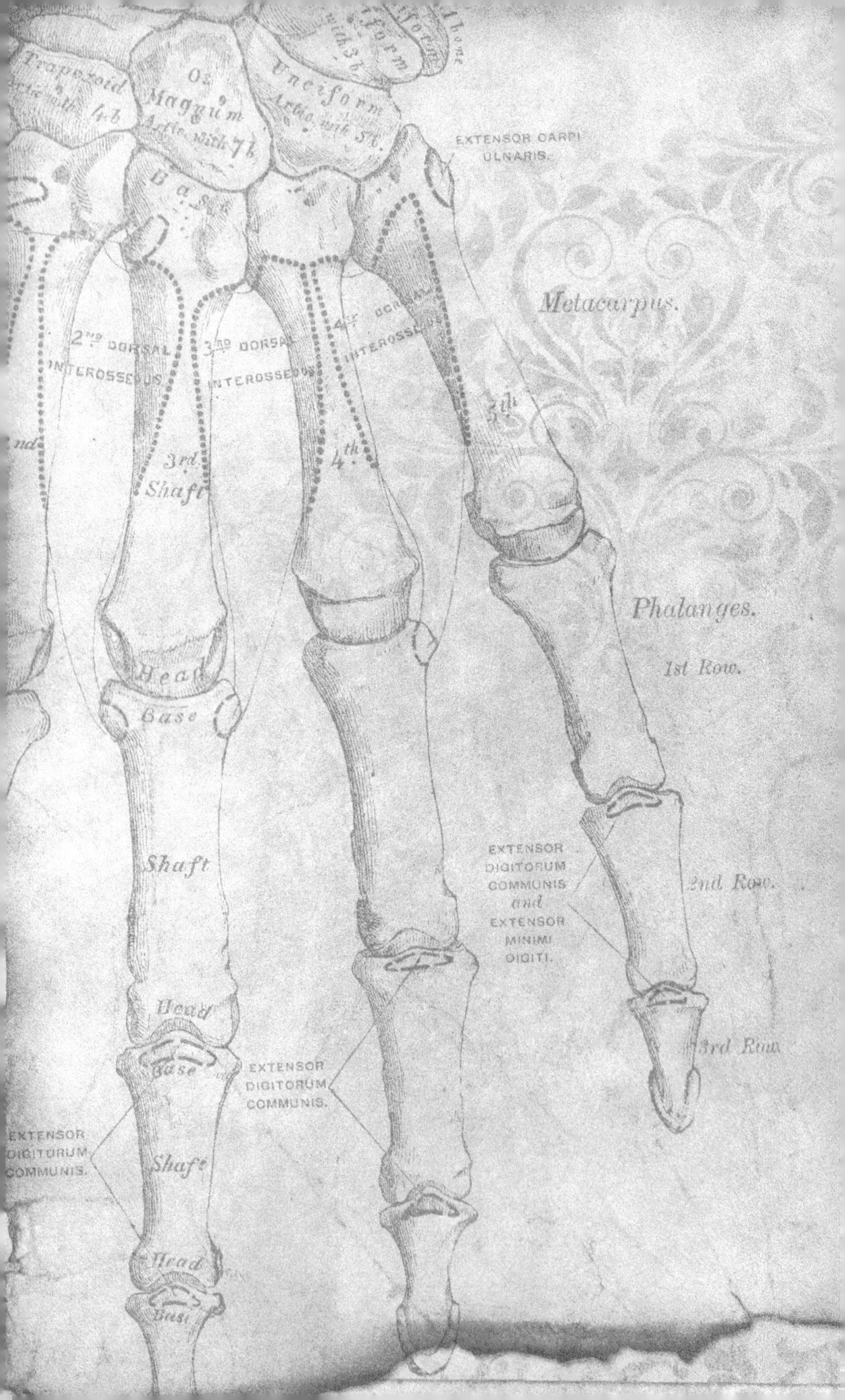

Trapezoid
Artic. with 4.b
Os Magnum Artic. with 7.b
Unciform Artic. with 5.c
Base
EXTENSOR CARPI ULNARIS.
Metacarpus.
2nd DORSAL INTEROSSEOUS
3rd DORSAL INTEROSSEOUS
4th DORSAL INTEROSSEOUS
3rd Shaft
4th
5th
Phalanges.
1st Row.
Head
Base
Shaft
EXTENSOR DIGITORUM COMMUNIS and EXTENSOR MINIMI DIGITI.
2nd Row.
Head
Base
EXTENSOR DIGITORUM COMMUNIS.
3rd Row
EXTENSOR DIGITORUM COMMUNIS.
Shaft
Head
Base

I should have seen the signs
Blinding, glaringly obvious
Like a canary in the coal mine
I should have noticed you were toxic from the start

I'm just a pair of quick lips
To check off your list

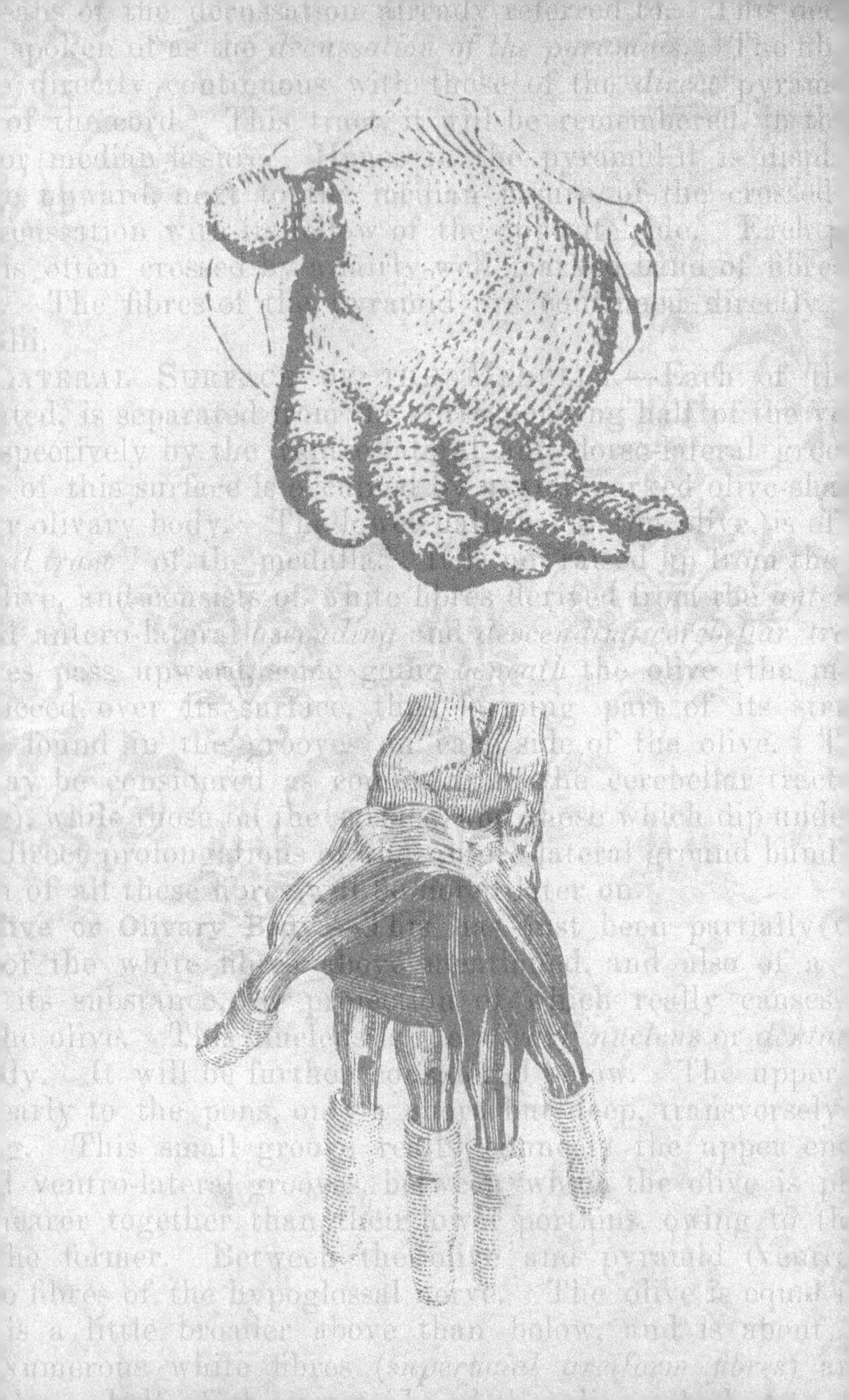

You're out of reach from the shoreline
Shark in the water
Blood on my hands
The unexpected undertow ripped you away from me

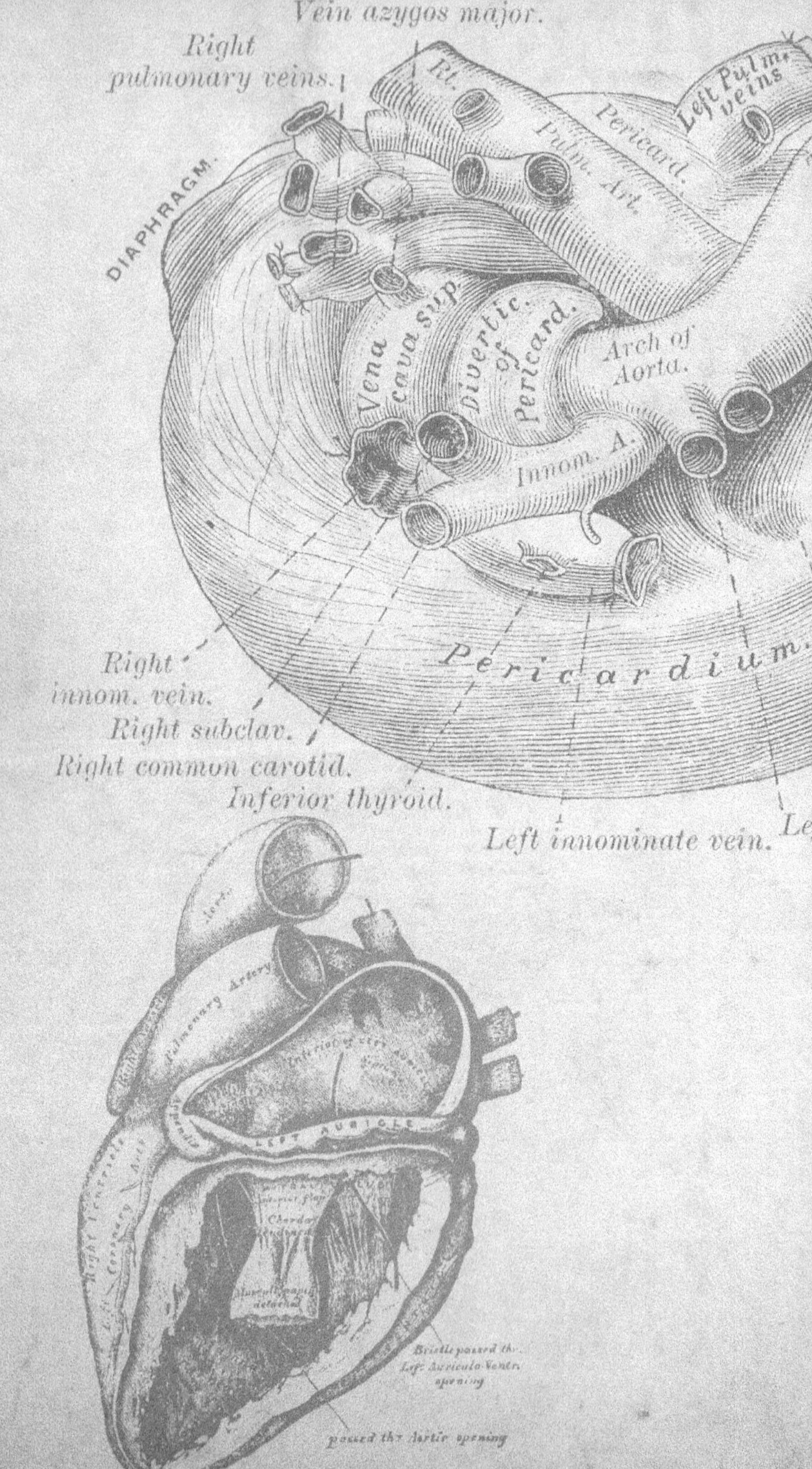

Vein azygos major.
Right pulmonary veins.
Rt.
Left Pulm. veins
Pericard.
Pulm. Art.
DIAPHRAGM.
Vena cava sup.
Divertic. of Pericard.
Arch of Aorta.
Innom. A.
Right innom. vein.
Right subclav.
Right common carotid.
Inferior thyroid.
Pericardium.
Left innominate vein. Lef
Aorta
Pulmonary Artery
Right Ventricle
LEFT AURICLE
Chordæ
Musculi papill. detached
Bristle passed th. Left Auriculo-Ventr. opening
passed th. Aortic opening

A graveyard of our relationship
Like a Slasher movie
You made a horror of it all
You took my heart
You buried it six feet under

the linea ilio-pectinea, and the upper margin of the symphysis pubis into the
and true pelvis.

The **false pelvis** is all that expanded portion of the pelvic cavity whic
situated above this plane. It is bounded on each side by the ossa ilii; in fro

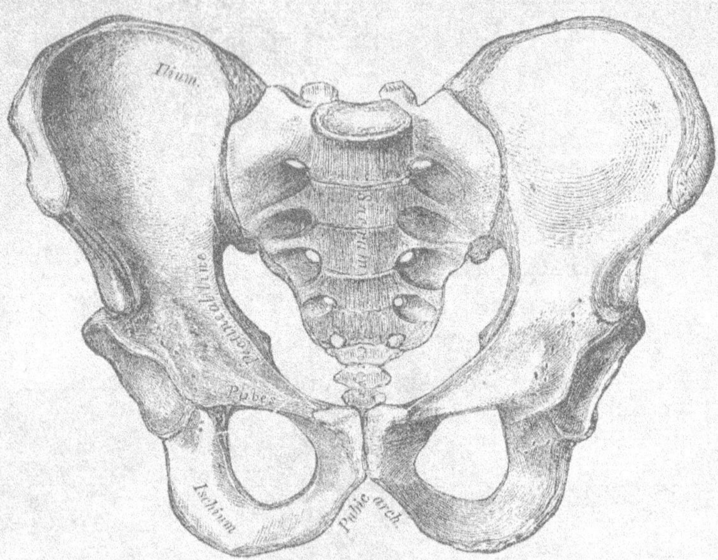

Fig. 210.—Male pelvis (adult).

is incomplete, presenting a wide interval between the spinous processes of the
on either side, which is filled up in the recent state by the parietes of the abdom

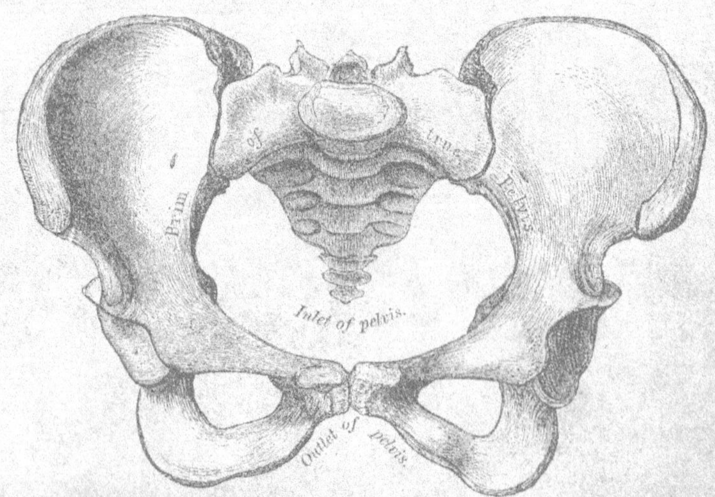

Fig. 211.—Female pelvis (adult).

behind, in the middle line, is a deep notch. This broad, shallow cavity is fit
to support the intestines and to transmit part of their weight to the anterior w
of the abdomen, and is, in fact, really a portion of the abdominal cavity.
term false pelvis is incorrect, and this space ought more properly to be regarded
part of the hypogastric region of the abdomen.

We can stand here all night
Battle of the wits
Sexual innuendos
Put your money where your mouth is
Let's kiss

I've got a silver tongue
Slashing skin and bone
With a quick wit,
I've sent better men than you to a shallow grave

with sufficient accuracy for all practical purposes ... cranium is
normally exposed by removing with the trephine a certain portion of the skull's area.
The various landmarks on the outside of the skull, which can be easily felt, and which

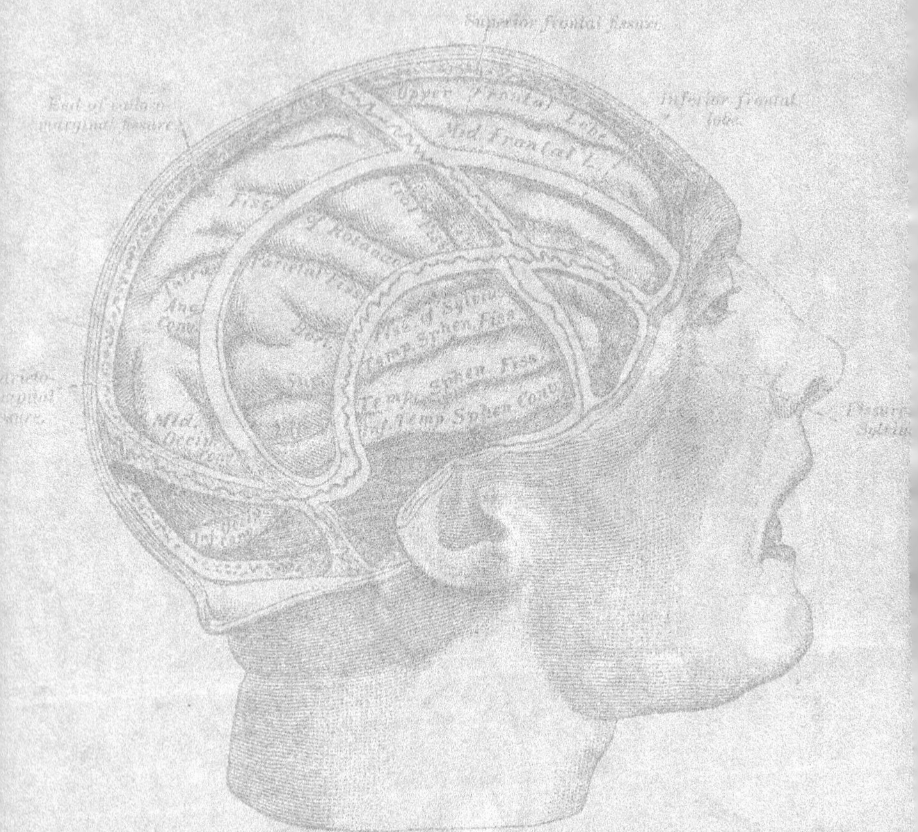

Fig. 46.—Drawing to illustrate cranio-cerebral topography. (Macalister.) Taken from a cast prepared ... fessor Cunningham

indications of the position of the parts beneath, have been already referred to (see page 28 ...). The relation of the fissures and convolutions to these landmarks is as follows:

Longitudinal Fissure.—This corresponds to a line drawn from the glabella at the root ... nose to the external occipital protuberance.

The Fissure of Sylvius.—The position of the fissure of Sylvius and its horizontal limb ... marked by a line starting from a point one inch and a quarter horizontally behind the external angular process of the frontal bone to a point three-quarters of an inch below the most prominent point of the parietal eminence. The first three-quarters of an inch will represent the ... are the remainder the horizontal limb. The bifurcation of the fissure is, therefore, ... a little behind and about a quarter of an inch above the level of the external angular process ... ascending limb of the fissure passes upward from this point parallel to, and immediately ... find, the coronal suture.

Fissure of Rolando.—To find the upper end of the fissure of Rolando a measurement ... should be taken from the glabella to the external occipital protuberance. The position of ... of the sulcus will be, measuring from in front, 55.6 per cent. of the whole distance from ... bella to the external occipital protuberance. Professor Thane adopts a somewhat simpler method. He divides the distance from the glabella to the external occipital protuberance ... top of the head into two equal parts, and, having thus defined the middle point of the ... he takes half an inch behind it as the top of the sulcus. This is not quite so accurate ... former method, but it is sufficiently so for all practical purposes, and on account of its ... ... is very generally adopted. From this point the fissure runs downward and forward for...

You're a face on a milk carton of my life.
I've been hanging missing person posters in my mind.
You're on my Most Wanted list
ghosting me: the crime

supracondylar line). The inner one (*internal supracondylar line*) is less marked, especially at its upper part, where it is crossed by the femoral artery. It terminates, below, at the summit of the internal condyle, in a small tubercle, the *Adductor tubercle*, which affords attachment to the tendon of the Adductor magnus.

To the inner lip of the linea aspera and its inner prolongation above and below is attached the Vastus internus, and to the outer lip and its outer prolongation above is attached the Vastus externus. The Adductor magnus is attached to the linea aspera, to its outer prolongation above and its inner prolongation below. Between the Vastus externus and the Adductor magnus are attached two muscles—viz. the Gluteus maximus above, and the short head of the Biceps below. Between the Adductor magnus and the Vastus internus four muscles are attached: the Iliacus and Pectineus above (the latter to the middle of the upper divisions); below these, the Adductor brevis and Adductor longus. The linea aspera is perforated a little below its centre by the nutrient canal, which is directed obliquely upward.

The *two lateral borders* of the femur are only slightly marked, the outer one extending from the anterior inferior angle of the great trochanter to the anterior extremity of the external condyle; the inner one from the spiral line, at a point opposite the trochanter minor, to the anterior extremity of the internal condyle. The internal border marks the limit of attachment of the Crureus muscle internally.

The anterior surface includes that portion of the shaft which is situated between the two lateral borders. It is smooth, convex, broader above and below than in the centre, slightly twisted, so that its upper part is

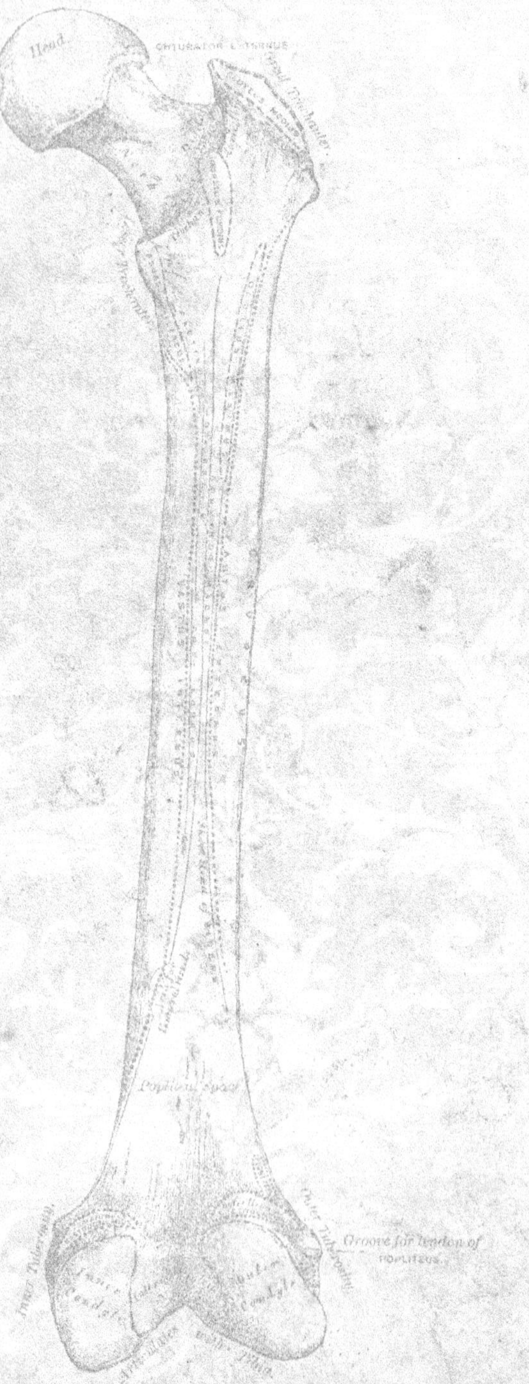

Fig. 214.—Right femur. Posterior surface.

My happiness drips away
with the sands in an hourglass
as I wait for you to return

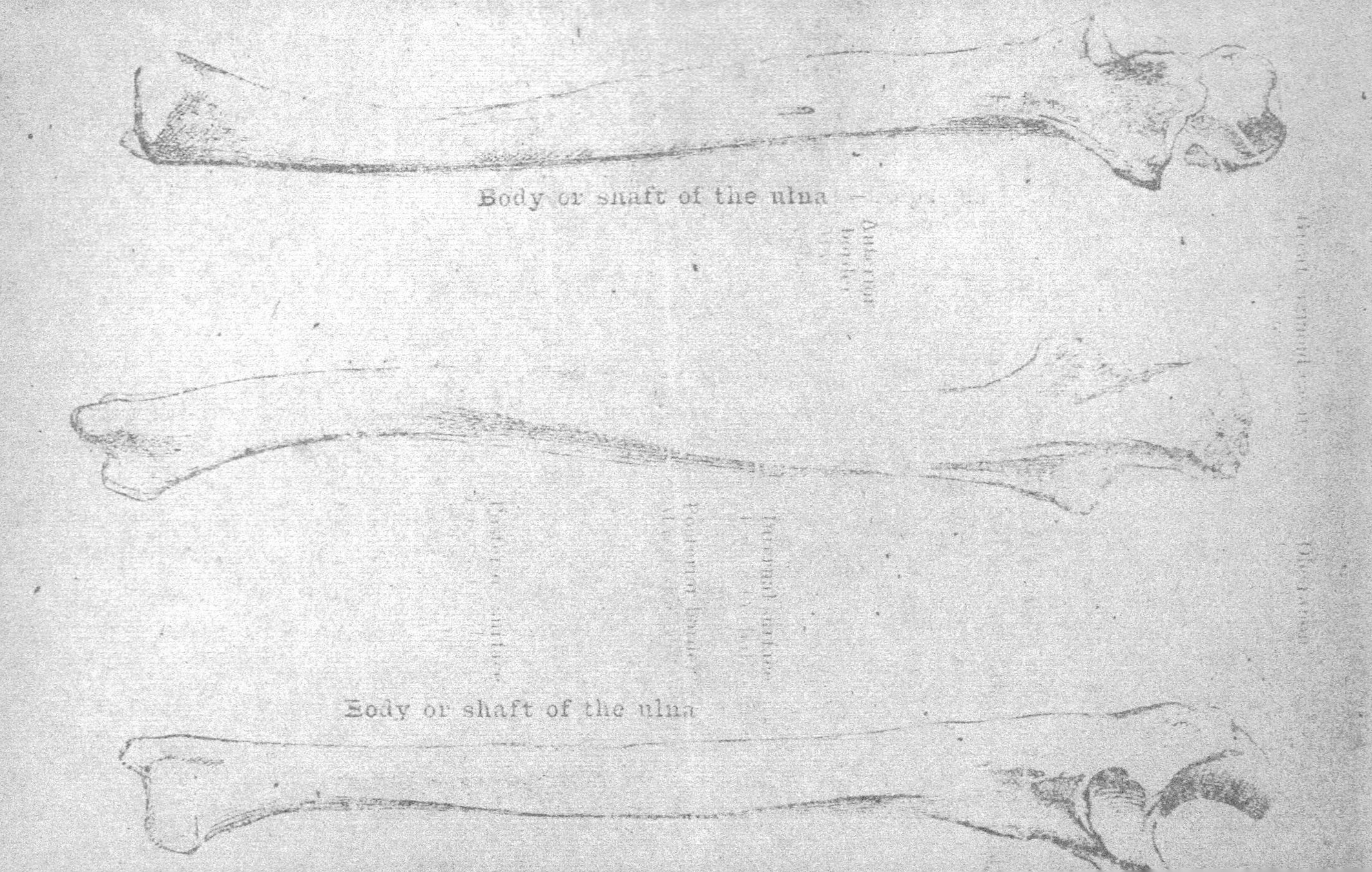
Body or shaft of the ulna
Anterior border
Internal surface
Posterior border
External surface
Body or shaft of the ulna

I am not myself
A lesser plastic version
Some vixen Barbie shell.
I look back and want to erase
Every memory, every touch.
To run from the Ken you've become

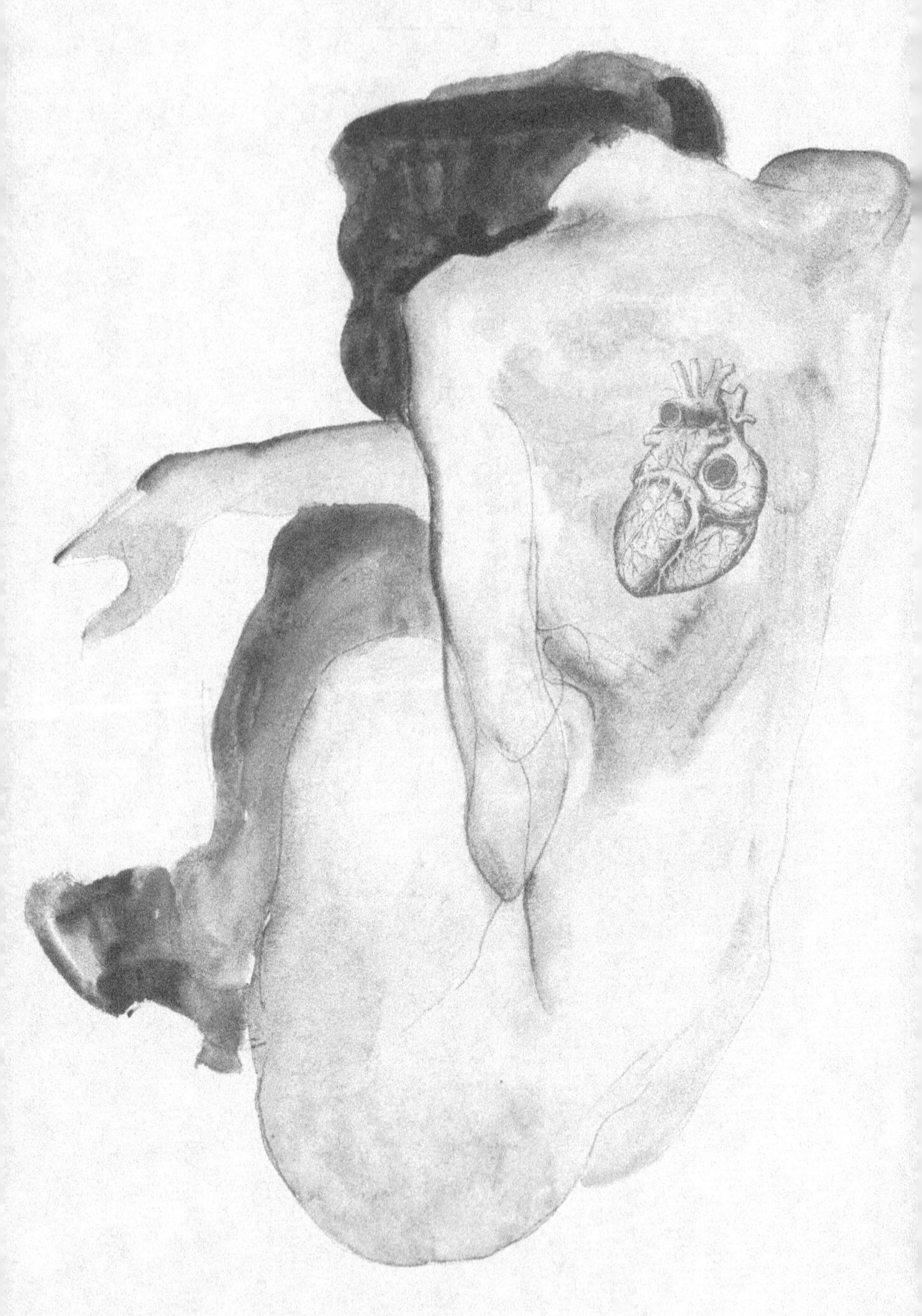

Exacerbated, Frustrated
To prove I'm numb
As numb as you've become
A Palace Guard
Frozen in silence
My heart shielded in a cover of pain

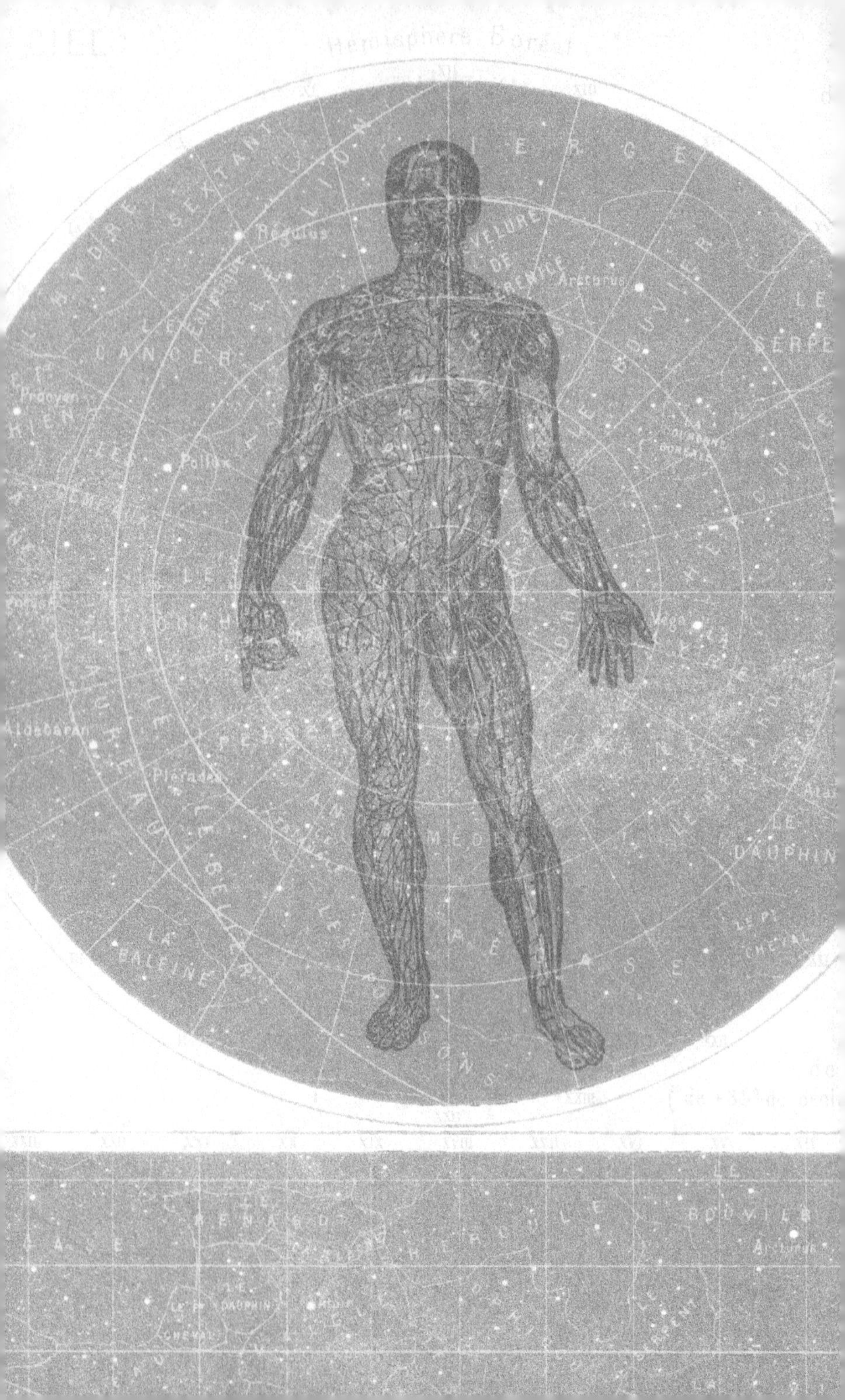

Hémisphère Boréal
HYDRE
SEXTANT
LE LION
Régulus
LA VIERGE
CHEVELURE DE BÉRÉNICE
HERCULE
Arcturus
LE BOUVIER
LE SERPE
LE CANCER
Procyon
LE CHIEN
Pollux
Aldébaran
Les Pléiades
PERSÉE
ANDROMÈDE
Véga
LE LÉZARD
Altaïr
LE DAUPHIN
LA BALEINE
LE PETIT CHEVAL
LE RENARD
BOUVIER
Arcturus
LE P. DAUPHIN
CHEVAL

When I look up at the night sky, all I see is you
Your body, so celestial, outlined in the constellations
The milky way your skin feels
The cosmos was made for me and you alone

...rior longitudinal sinus.
...terior meningeal artery.
Foramen cæcum.
Crista galli.
Slit for nasal nerve.
Groove for nasal nerve.
...terior ethmoidal foramen.
...ices for olfactory nerves.
...rior ethmoidal foramen.
Ethmoidal spine.
Olfactory groove.
Optic foramen.
Optic groove.
Olivary process.
Anterior clinoid process.
Middle clinoid process.
Posterior clinoid process.
Groove for 6th nerve.
Foramen lacerum medium.
Orifice of carotid canal.
...for Gasserian ganglion.
Meatus auditorius internus.
Slit for dura mater.
Superior petrosal groove.
Foramen lacerum posterius.
Anterior condyloid foramen.
Aquæductus vestibuli.
Posterior condyloid foramen.
Foramen magnum.
Mastoid foramen.
Posterior meningeal groove.

Anterior Fossa
Orbital Plate of Frontal
Body & Lesser Wing of Sphenoid
Great Wing of Sphenoid
Middle Fossa
Petrous Portion of Temporal
Posterior Fossa
Occipital
for Lateral Sinus

Base of the skull. Inner or cerebral surface.

Daisy chains link our memories

parallel with one another, and directed obliquely downward and backward. Externally it is covered by the parotid gland and by the integument. Internal-

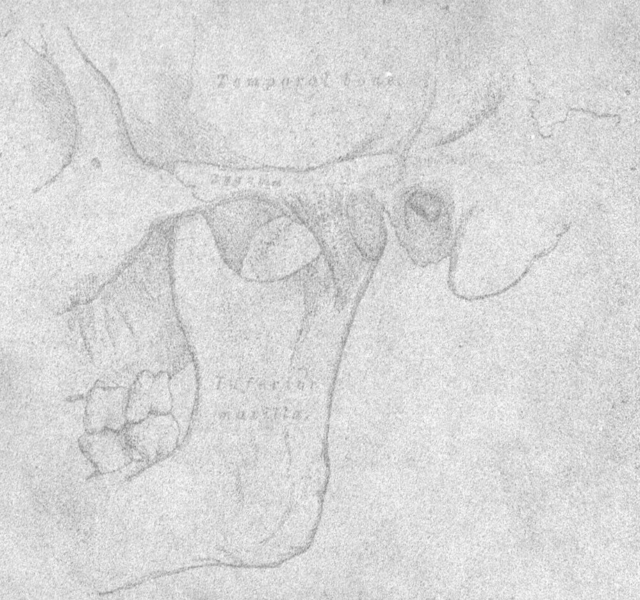

Fig. —Temporo-maxillary articulation. External view.

it is in relation with the capsular ligament, of which it is an accessory band, and not separable from it.

The Internal Lateral Ligament (Fig.) is a specialized band of cervical fascia which is attached above to the spinous process of the sphenoid bone, and, becoming broader as it descends, is inserted into the lingula and margin of the dental foramen. Its outer surface is in relation above, with the External pterygoid muscle; lower down, it is separated from the neck of the condyle by the Internal maxillary artery; and still more internally, the inferior dental vessels and nerve separate it from the ramus of the jaw. The inner surface is in relation with the Internal pterygoid.

The Stylo-maxillary Ligament is also a specialized band of the cervical fascia, which extends from near the apex of the styloid process of the temporal bone to the

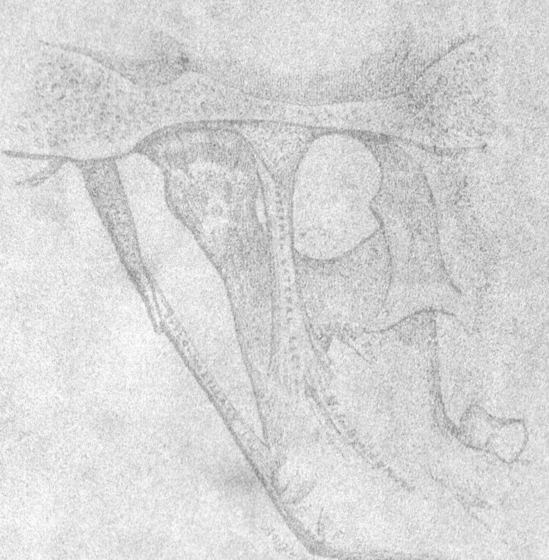

Fig. —Temporo-maxillary articulation. Internal view.

angle and posterior border of the ramus of the lower jaw, between the Masseter and Internal pterygoid muscles. This ligament separates the parotid from the submaxillary gland, and has attached to its inner side part of the fibres of origin of the Stylo-glossus muscle. Although usually classed among the ligaments of the jaw, it can only be considered as an accessory in the articulation.

Tell me a story of your childhood
How you conquered pirates and monsters
Traveled the seven seas and walked the moon
Of all the little memories that made you who you are

Your love comes like the tide
In waves
Slipping away and all-encompassing floods
Never enough
Just enough
Never too much
Before drifting all too fast out of reach

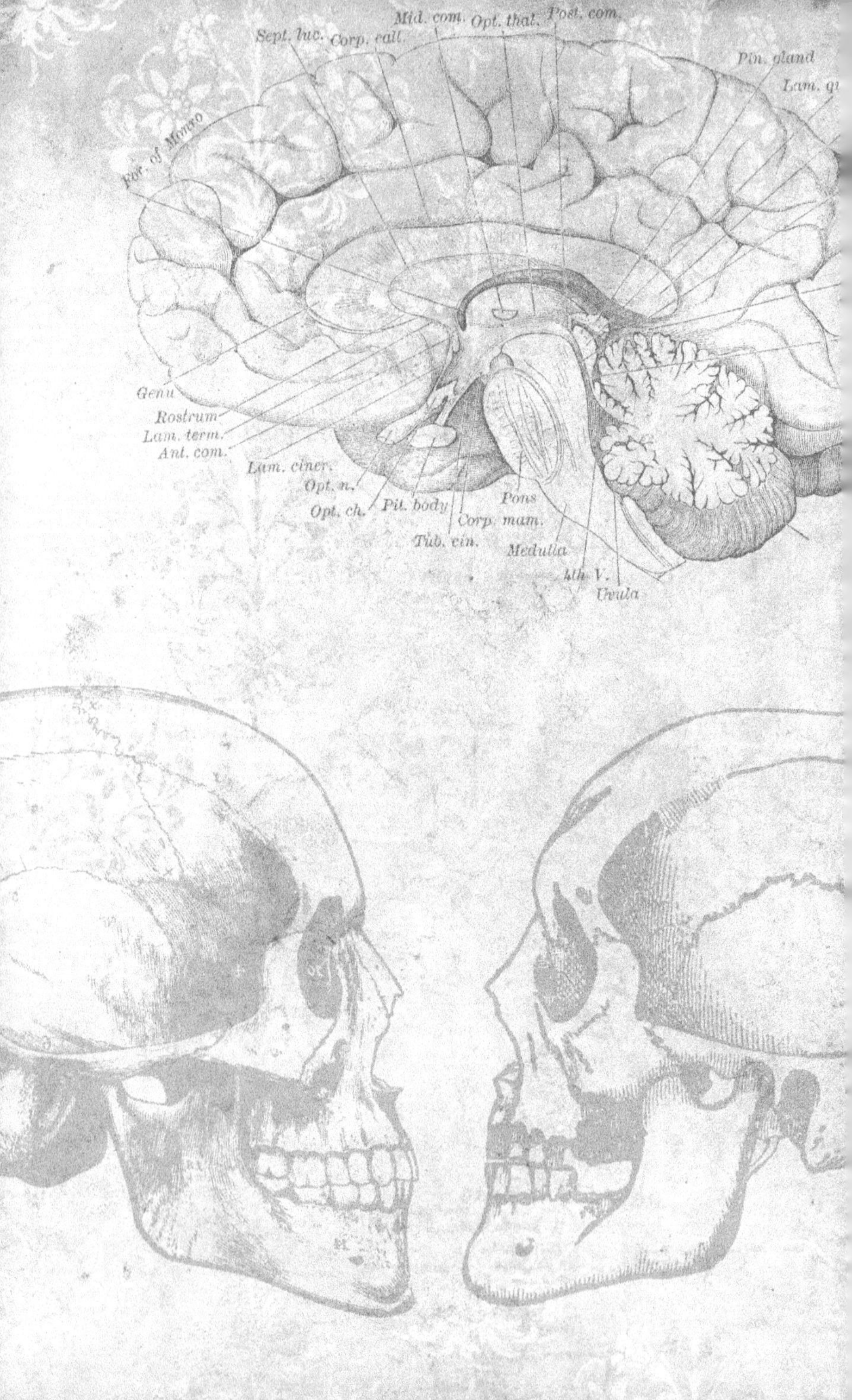

Sept. luc.
Corp. call.
Mid. com.
Opt. that.
Post. com.
Pin. gland
Lam. qu
For. of Monro
Genu
Rostrum
Lam. term.
Ant. com.
Lam. ciner.
Opt. n.
Opt. ch.
Pit. body
Tub. cin.
Pons
Corp. mam.
Medulla
4th V.
Uvula

Kiss me like you mean it
Kill the lights
Get close
Let our bodies touch
Feel the humming of the unknowing
I can feel your breath intertwining with mine
Peppermint gum and cheap beer
Let's get lost in the bedsheets

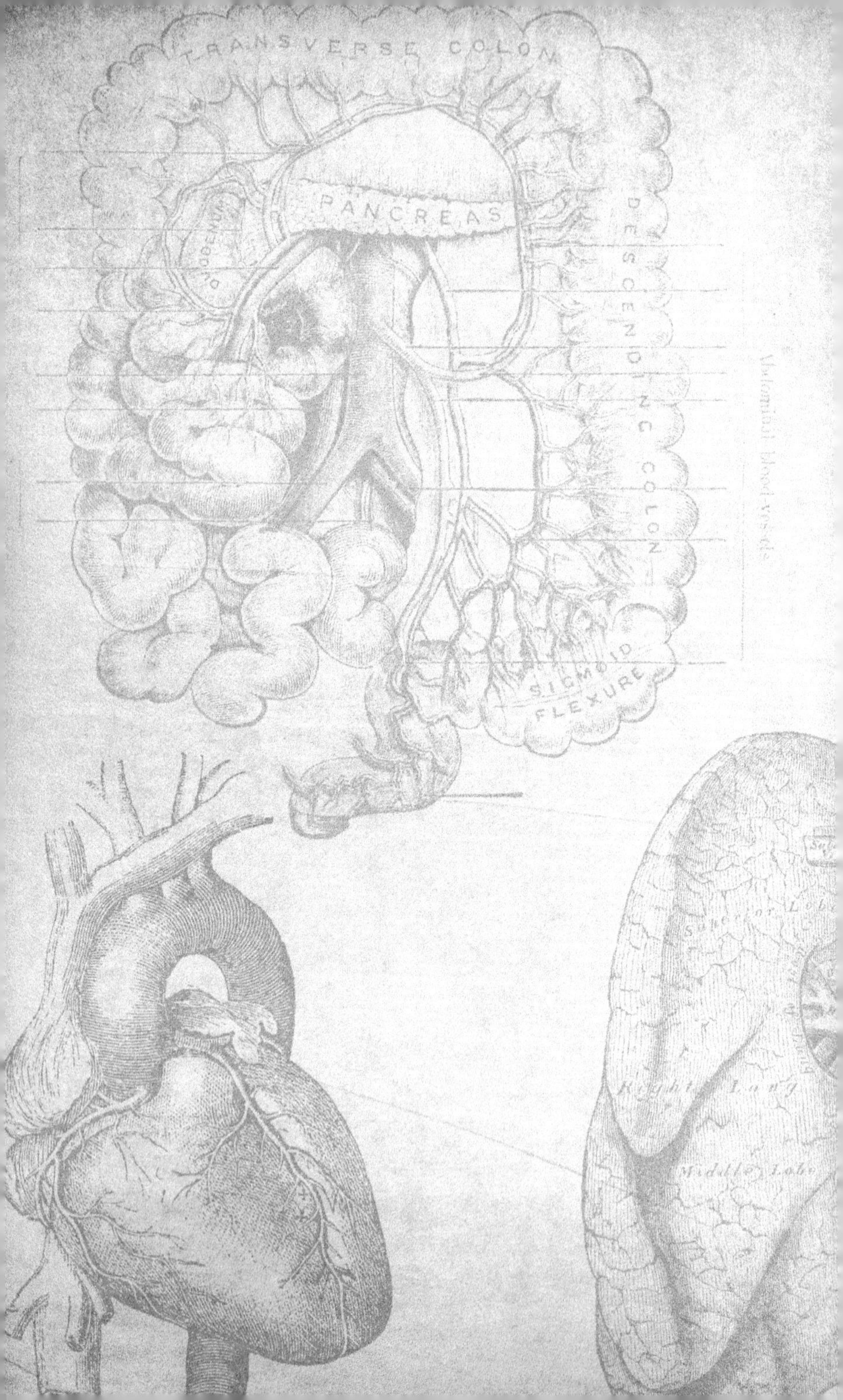

TRANSVERSE COLON
PANCREAS
DUODENUM
DESCENDING COLON
Abdominal Blood-vessels
SIGMOID FLEXURE
Superior Lobe
Right Lung
Middle Lobe

Always in
Back of my mind
Deep in my gut
Part of my heart

Bazas, le 28 avril 1908

Cher Monsieur Deslandes

Vos remèdes ont-ils [guéri?]
ri une entérite chronique ?
Voulez vous les essayer
de la charité de mon hôpital.
[...] de 35 à 40 ans. On l'opère
[...] et on la laissera, en [...]

There might be an elephant in the room
But it feels more like a tiger in a cage

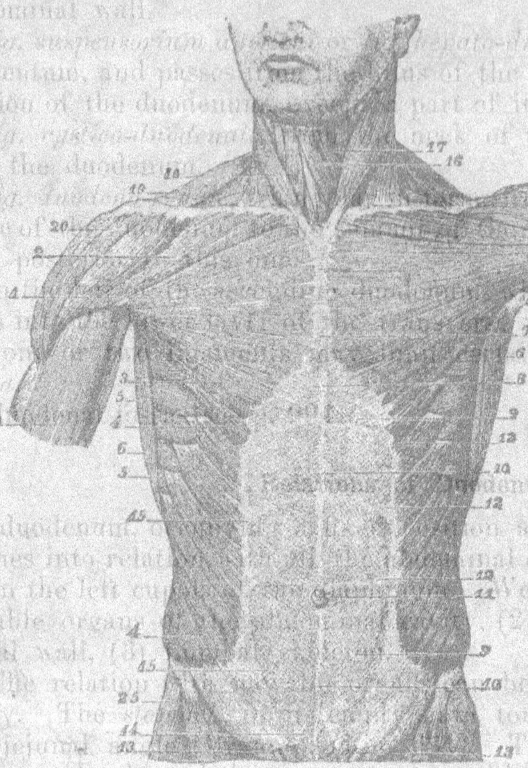

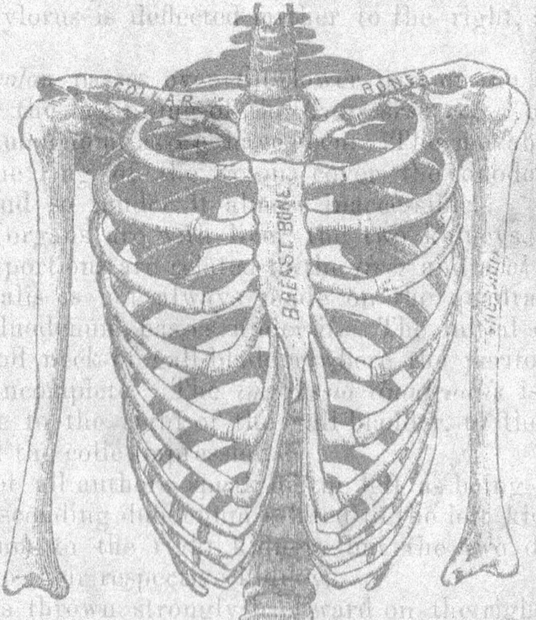

COLLAR BONE

BREAST BONE

BONES

I know that deep dark depression when you're a stranger in your skin that becomes more familiar than yourself.
I have breathed its intoxicating fog.
Then I learned the warm embrace of love that tingles in the tips of your fingers and behind your ears.
I try to get back to the purr of the cat and the smell of his cologne that lingers on his day-old shirt.
Everyday moments bleed into my soul deeper still.

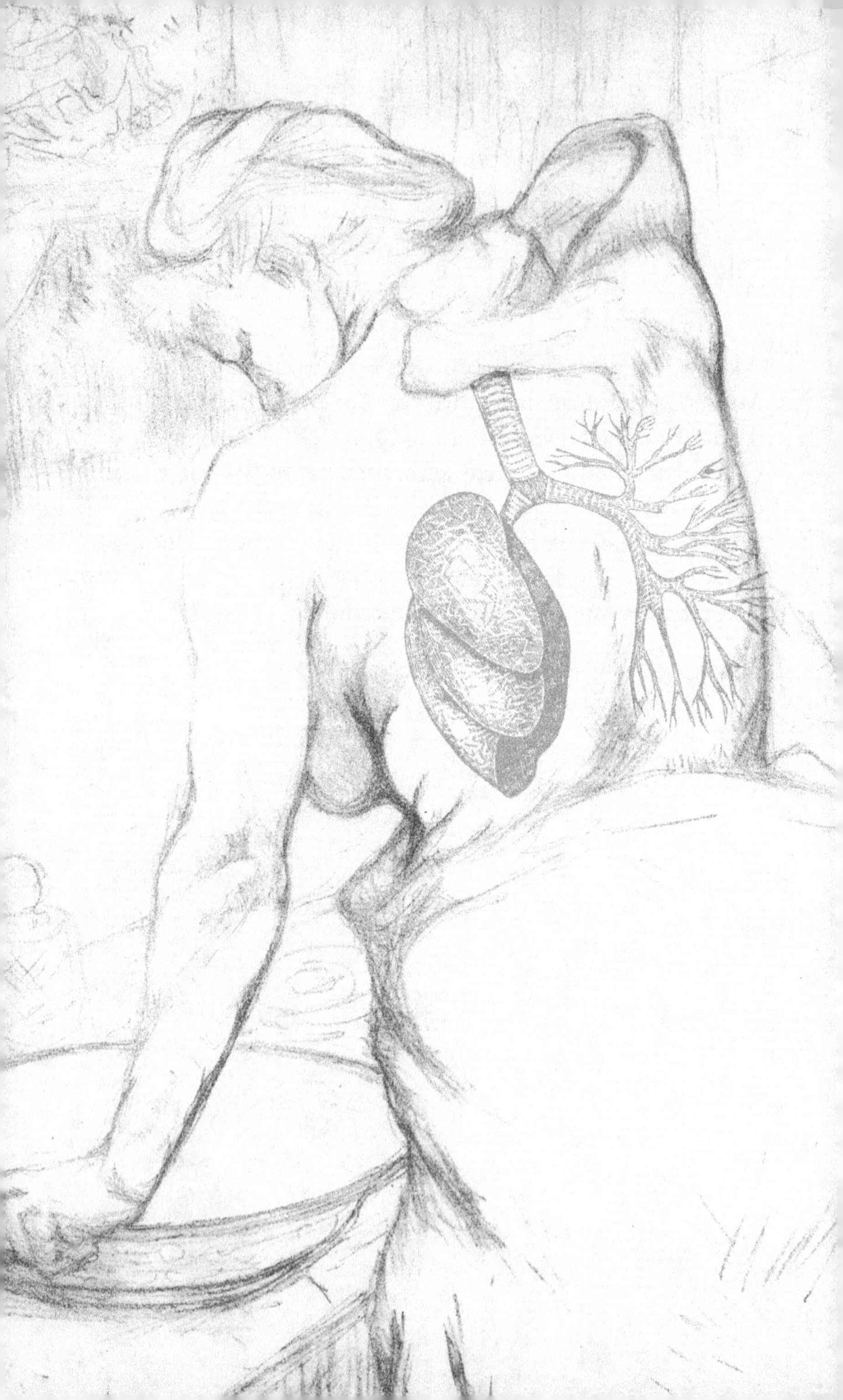

Demons' wicked whispers,
Their words lapping at my ears
Reminding me of every lie you've ever said:
I'm weak
I'm faking it
I'm too negative

The Wilderness whispers through the forest.
Telling me stories of those who have come and who shall follow.
The soil under my feet holds secrets
Of everything that's walked my path.
The coming blossoms hold the promise of tomorrow.
The sun kisses my cheeks upon daybreak
Gently reminding me to breathe in the eternity of this moment.

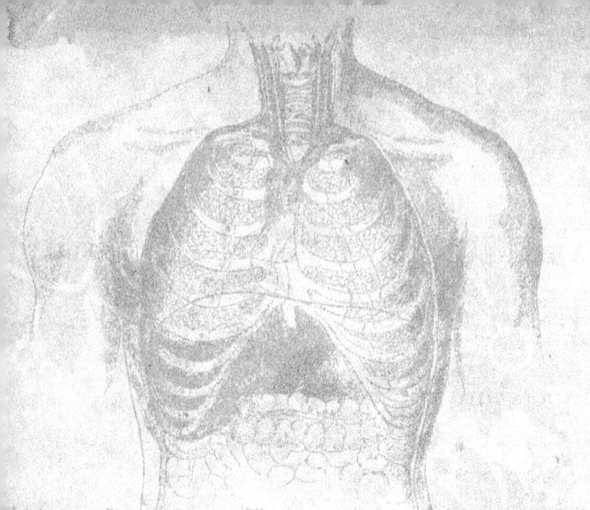

internal surface (Fig. 155) is unequally divided into two parts b[y a]
rojection of bone, the *palate process*: the portion above the palat[e]

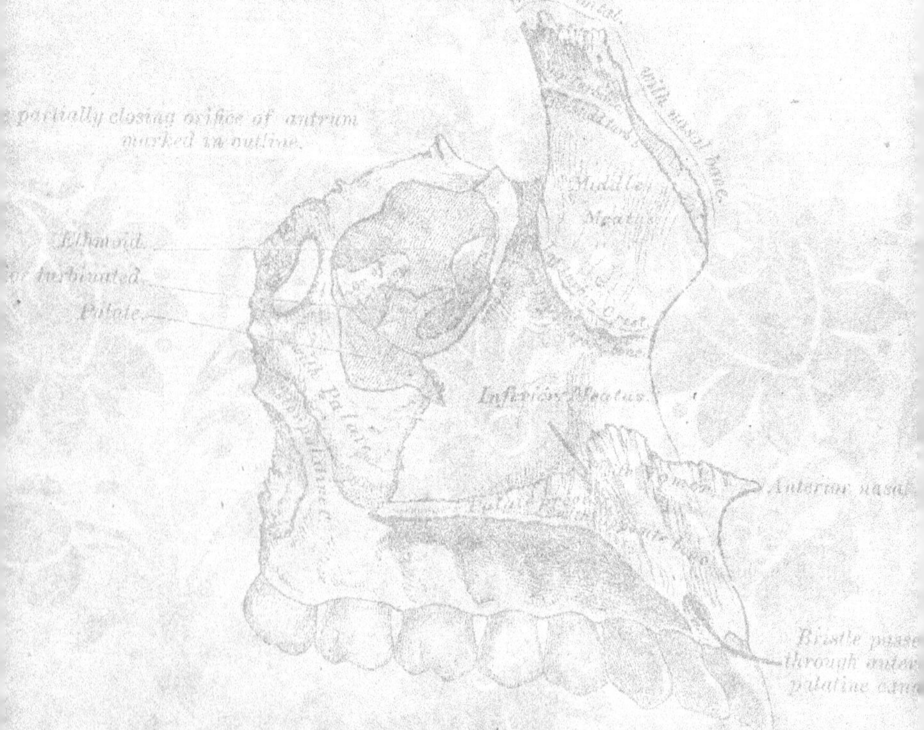

Fig. 155.—Left superior maxillary bone. Internal surface

[par]t of the outer wall of the nasal fossæ; that below it forms par[t of]
the mouth. The superior division of this surface presents a larg[e open]-
[in]g leading into the *antrum of Highmore*. At the upper border[s]

How is it that even now
As I read back your words
My breath catches
at the slightest caress
your promises bring

The lateral ventricles are the cavities of the hemispheres, each [...] the other. In each hemisphere the lateral ventricle is situate[d ...] inner regions, being surrounded above, in front and externally, [...] the white matter of the hemisphere. Each lateral ventricle [...] through the foramen of Monro with the third ventricle, and is li[ned ...] a thin membrane (the *ependyma*), covered by nucleated ep[ithelium ...] scattered here and there in patches. It is moistened by [...] which is sometimes, even in health, secreted in considerable quant[ity ...] separated from the other by a vertical septum, the *septum lucidum*.

Each lateral ventricle consists (Fig. 445) of a central cav[ity ...] and three accessory ca[vities ...] *cornua*. The *anterior* [...] forward and outward [...] stance of the frontal l[obe ...] prises that portion of [...] which is anterior to the [...] Monro. The *body* o[r ...] portion of the ventric[le ...] between the foramen [...] the posterior part of [...] lamina. It is situated [...] the parietal lobe. By [...] rior extremity diverges [...] lowing. The *posterior* [...] the *digital cavity*, pas[ses ...] into the occipital lobe [...] *cornu* descends into [...] lobe.

If the upper part [...] spheres is removed [...] inch above the level [...] callosum, the internal [...] will be exposed. I[t ...] shaped centre, of whi[ch ...] surrounded on all side[s ...] convoluted margin of [...] which presents an app[earance ...] nearly every part. I[f ...] real mass has been cut [...] [...] Its surface is studded with numerous minute red [...]

Fig. 445.—The right lateral ventricle laid open from above [...]

And I felt the weight of grief
Pull me under
Swallow me whole
And I sat there in it
Allowing it to wash over me
Holding me in its totality.

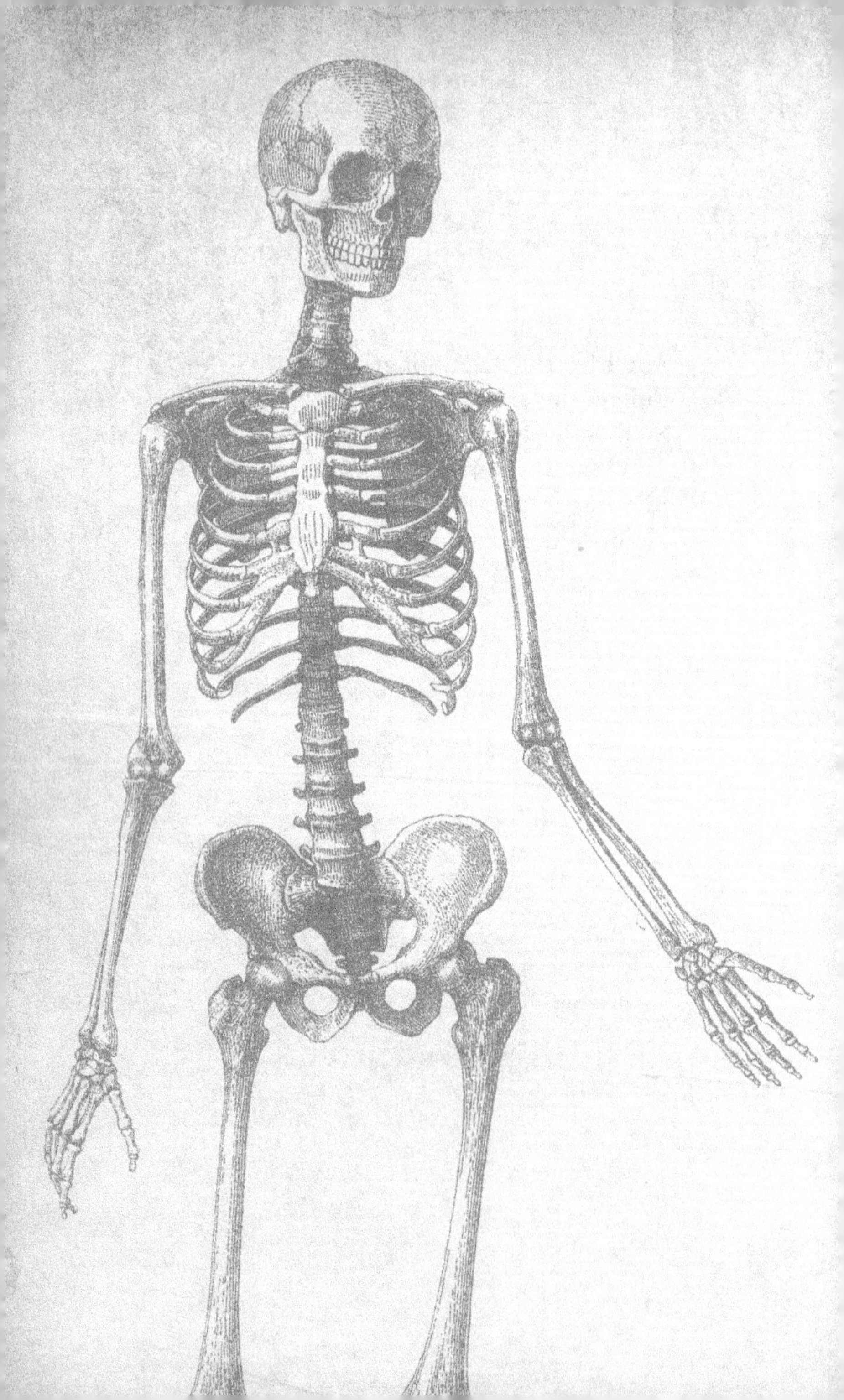

The darkness is back,
And it has cracked my ribs.
Breaking them into a million pieces,
Impossible to put it back together,
But so easy to watch them fall apart.
The hole is gapping.
Swollen and pulsating with emptiness.
Gnawing at my soul,
To give in to the pain that I've tucked away,
In the recess of my mind.

delate,

our minds light as we think

graduate!

dreams of angel white, wh

flowers

ned (not by myself of course) as

was ours

ein the at us know how

eems

with life's mysteries lives, and

streams

ghts are but the words

the left,

covers of

go by,

the dangers over, never fa

worldly news,

a look around

A sailor's knot is choking me
Salty waves crash down my cheeks
Swallowed whole by an ocean of uncertainty

THE MEDULLA OBLONGATA (Figs. 415 and 416).

General Description

[illegible] oblongata, or *spinal bulb*, is the first division of [illegible] below upwards. It has two extremities, superior and [illegible] dorsal, ventral, and two lateral. The inferior extremity [illegible] the spinal cord; the upper has a similarly direct [illegible] (Fig. 415). The surfaces in the upper half of the [illegible] other: in the lower half each runs into the other.

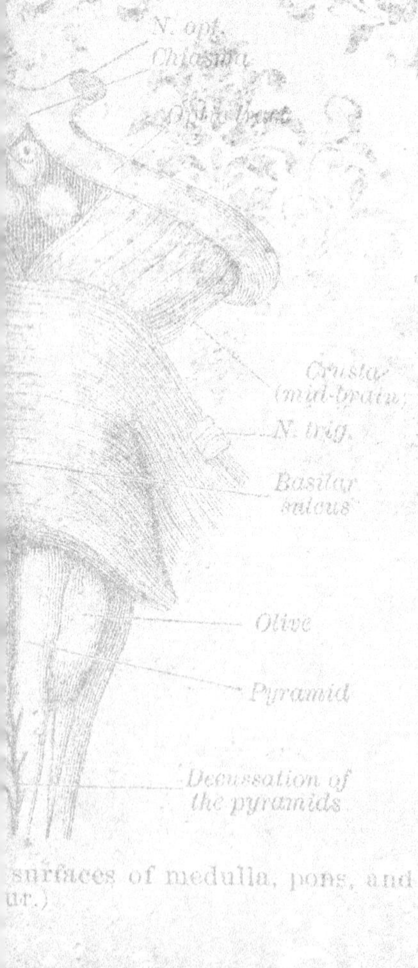

surfaces of medulla, pons, and [illegible]

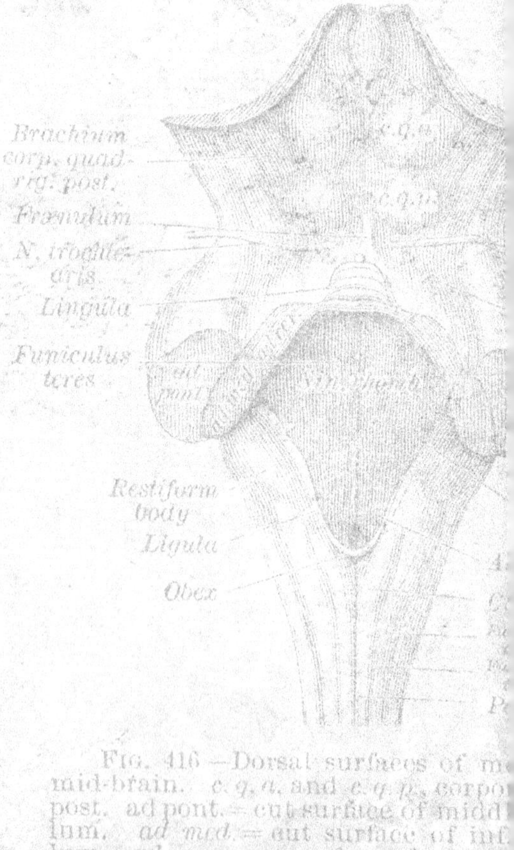

FIG. 416.—Dorsal surfaces of me[illegible] mid-brain. *c. q. a.* and *c. q. p.*, corpo[illegible] post. *ad pont.* = cut surface of midd[illegible] lum. *ad med.* = cut surface of inf[illegible] lum. *ad cer.* = cut surface of sup. p[illegible]

Melancholy blue,
a flitting bird on the windowsill
Escapism
A lonely heart
mimicking, mirroring,
the jay as it hops

III

Queen of the Jokers
Of the lost and abused
Have nothing to hold onto
No diamonds or hearts
Just loneliness in spades

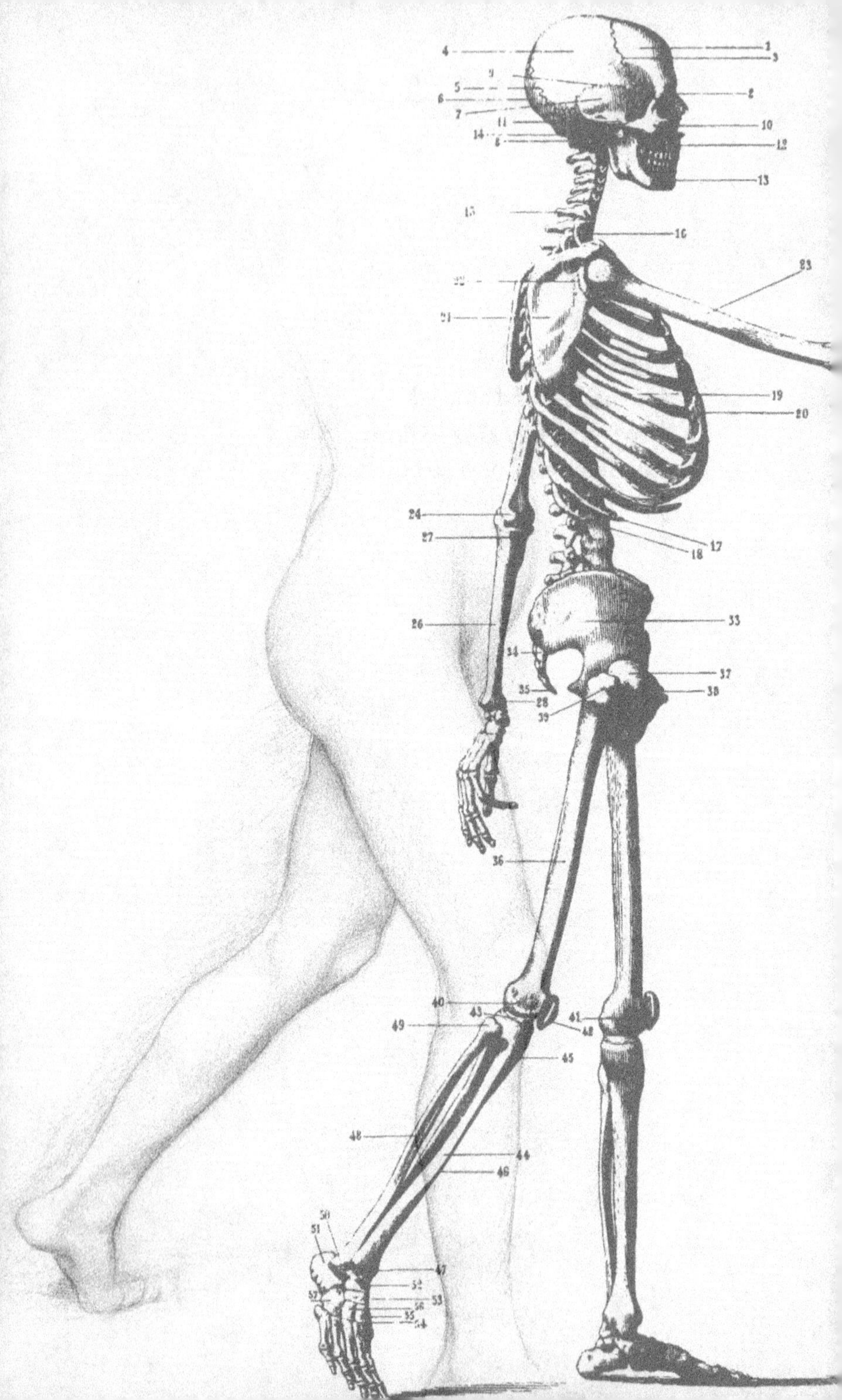

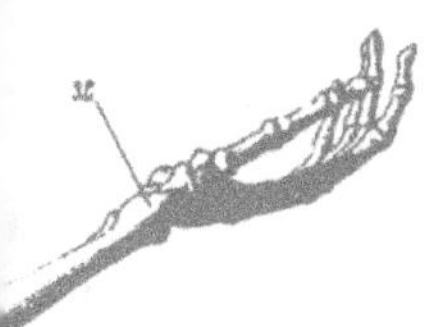

The agony of it all
The broken-down body
The loneliness
Traces my outline like a seductive lover
Coaxing me to her
Breathing pain into my lungs, burning as I inhale
The misery of it all
Like a passionate tango
Dragging me across the dance floor,
an unwilling partner

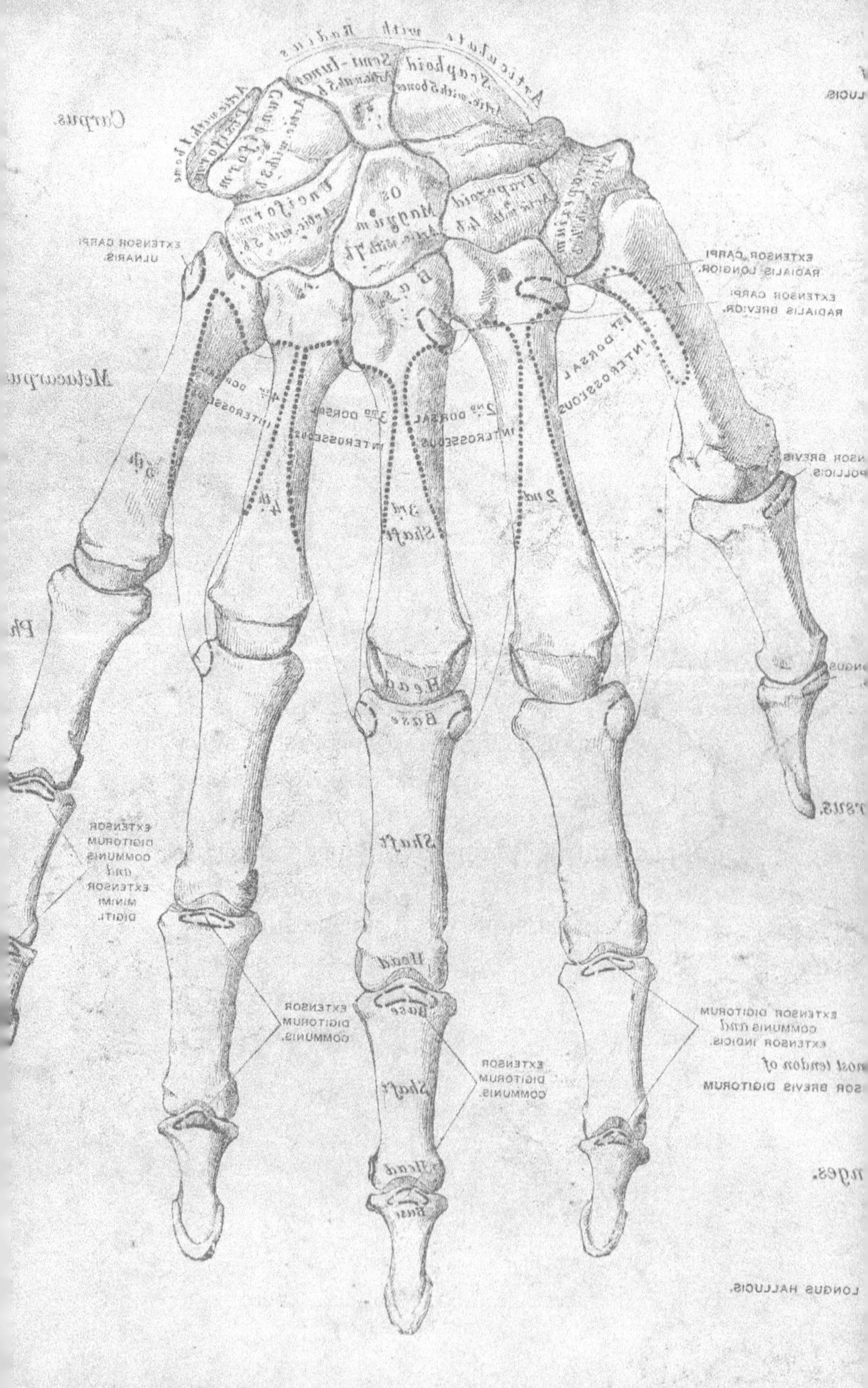

The dirt and grit underneath my fingernails grind deeper as I claw at the coffin.
Risen from the undead of my depression.
I smell the soil of life and love, and everything in between invades my senses.
It rips me from a lifeless corpse, from a numbness that left me plagued with the nothingness that death brings.

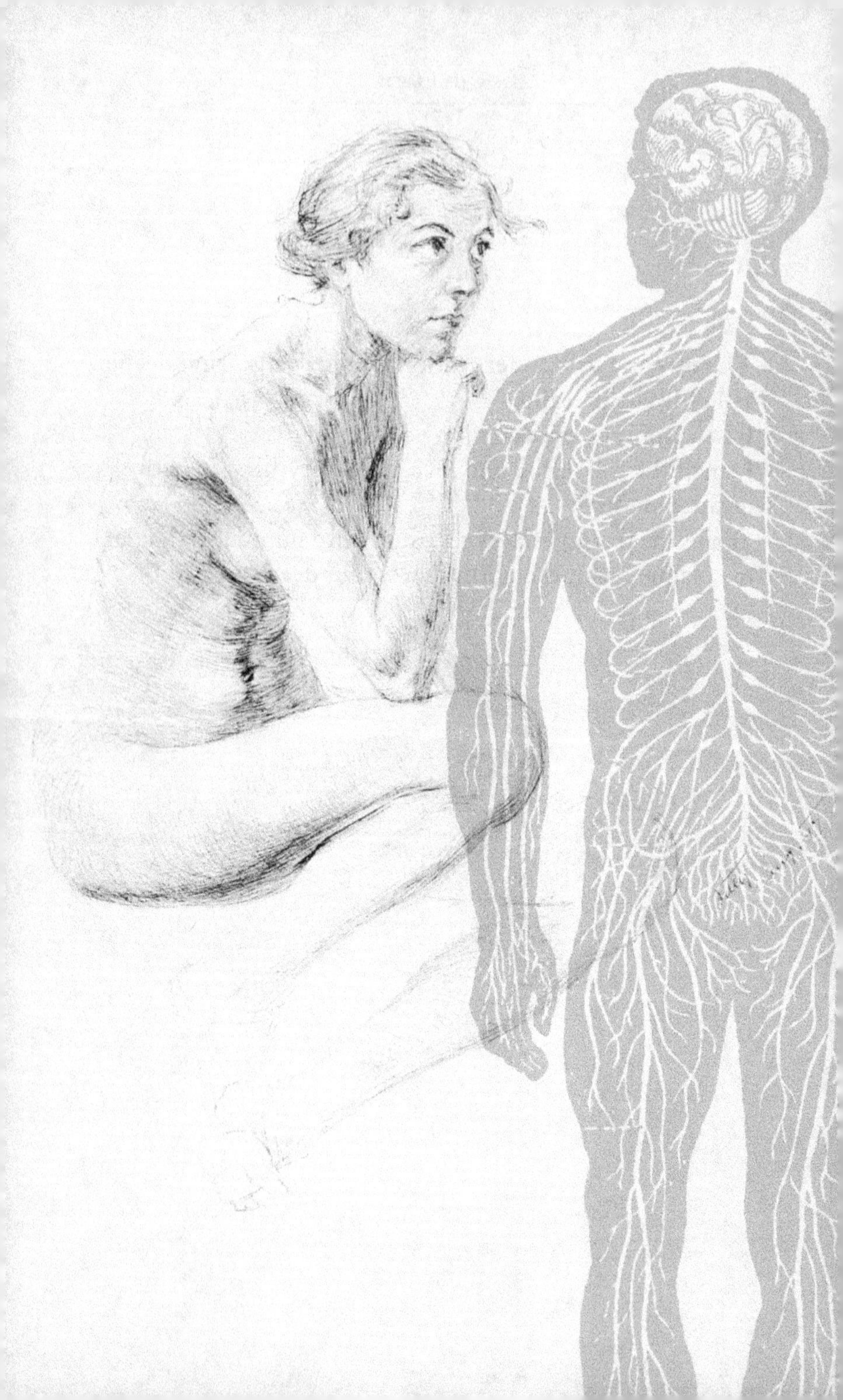

Fighting to find common ground
To Find my footing
Lost in my head
I miss what you're saying when I concentrate
So hard on the way your mouth moves
What did you just say?

anterior third of the fossa which is smooth, is covered by, but does not a[fford]
attachment to the fibres of this muscle. The venter is separated from [the]
posterior border by a smooth, triangular margin at the superior and inf[erior]
angles, and in the interval between these by a narrow edge which is often defin[ed].
This marginal surface affords attachment throughout its entire extent to [the]
Serratus magnus muscle. The subscapular fossa presents a transverse depre[ssion]
at its upper part, where the bone appears to be bent on itself, forming a consi[der]-
able angle, called the *subscapular angle*, thus giving greater strength to the [body]
of the bone from its arched form, while the summit of the arch serves to sup[port]
the spine and acromion process. It is in this situation that the fossa is dee[pest],
so that the thickest part of the Subscapularis muscle lies in a line perpendic[ular]
to the plane of the glenoid cavity, and must consequently operate most effectiv[ely]
on the head of the humerus, which is contained in that cavity.

The posterior surface, or dorsum (Fig. 135), is arched from above downw[ards],
alternately concave and convex from side to side. It is subdivided unequally [by]

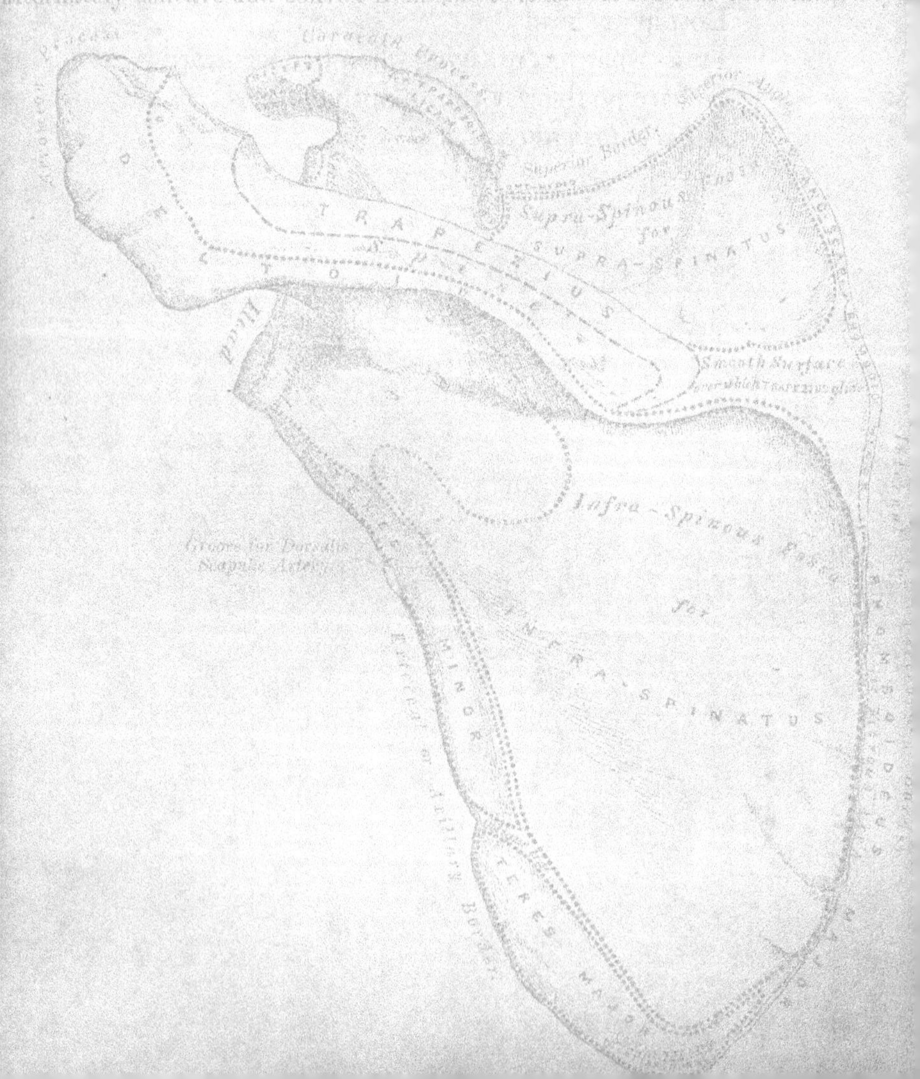

Anger piercing through the air
Your voice hitting octaves high above the cityscape
Drowning out everything around us
A force of nature yet so unnatural
My gut-churning from fear
Cowering away from the fury
Swirling, whirling, twirling
Your words dripping acid into my skin

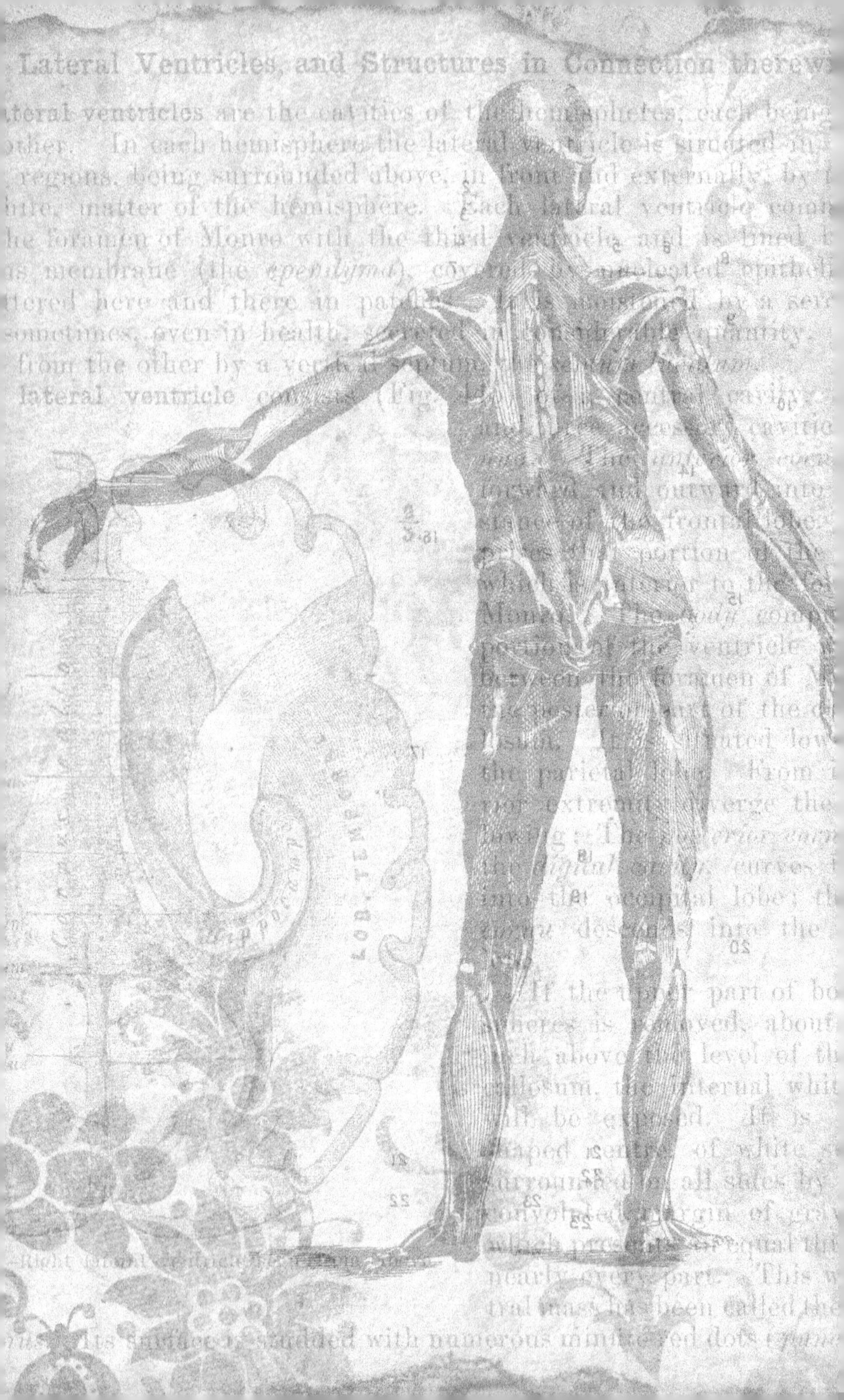

lateral ventricles are the cavities of the hemispheres, each being
other. In each hemisphere the lateral ventricle is situated in
regions, being surrounded above, in front and externally by
white matter of the hemisphere. Each lateral ventricle com
the foramen of Monro with the third ventricle and is lined
its membrane (the *ependyma*), covered by a nucleated epithel
tered here and there in patches, is sometimes by a ser
sometimes even in health, several in each ventricle,
from the other by a vertical septum the *septum lucidum*
lateral ventricle consists (Fig. —) of a central cavity
and forward and outward into
stance of the frontal lobe
the proportion of the
which is anterior to the
Monro. The *body* com
portion of the ventricle
between the foramen of
the posterior part of the
sium. Each situated low
the parietal lobe. From
rior extremity diverge the
having a The *posterior corn*
the *digital* cavity curves
into the occipital lobe; th
cornu descends into the

If the upper part of bo
heres is removed, about
inch above the level of th
callosum, the internal whit
will be exposed. It is
shaped centre of white
surrounded on all sides by
convoluted margin of grey
which presents nearly the
nearly every part. This w
tral mass has been called the
its surface is studded with numerous minute red dots (*puncta*

This is no paper cut
You buried the hatchet in my back
No peace between us
The weight of it all brings me crashing to my knees
Judas.
Brutus.
A true Benedict Arnold.
With no remorse, you plunge the ax deep.

supracondylar lines. The inner one (internal supracondylar line) is less marked, especially at its upper part, where it is crossed by the femoral artery. It terminates below, at the summit of the internal condyle, in a small tubercle, the Adductor tubercle, which affords attachment to the tendon of the Adductor magnus.

To the inner lip of the linea aspera and its inner prolongation above and below is attached the Vastus internus, and to the outer lip and its outer prolongation above is attached the Vastus externus. The Adductor magnus is attached to the linea aspera, to its outer prolongation above and its inner prolongation below. Between the Vastus externus and the Adductor magnus are attached two muscles—viz. the Gluteus maximus above, and the short head of the Biceps below. Between the Adductor magnus and the Vastus internus four muscles are attached: the Iliacus and Pectineus above (the latter to the middle of the upper division); below these, the Adductor brevis and Adductor longus. The linea aspera is perforated a little below its centre by the nutrient canal, which is directed obliquely upward.

The two lateral borders of the femur are only slightly marked, the outer one extending from the anterior inferior angle of the great trochanter to the anterior extremity of the external condyle; the inner one from the spiral line, at a point opposite the trochanter minor (the anterior extremity) to the internal condyle. The internal border marks the limit of attachment of the Crureus muscle internally.

The anterior surface includes that portion of the shaft which is situated between the two lateral borders. It is smooth, convex, broader above and below than in the centre, slightly twisted, so that its upper part is

Right femur. Posterior surface.

*A single flashing light in an abyss
where fiction has been blurred with fact.*

...illoni, D. Litt.

...MA . TEL. 365.682

C.I.

Mounds of Rolling flesh
Dips and slopes
Valleys and Peaks
Supple; awoken by your touch

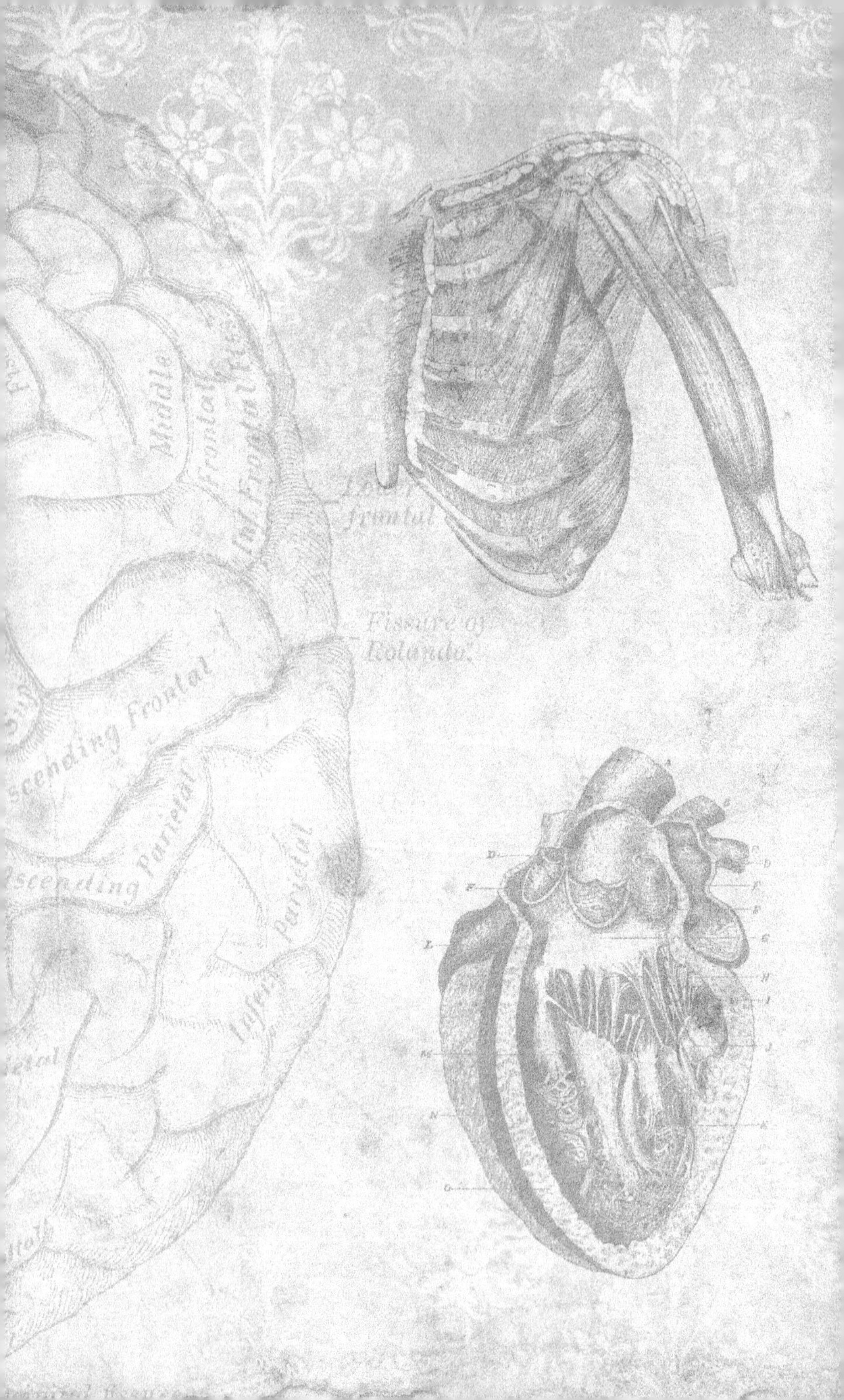

Middle Frontal
Inf. Frontal
Ascending Frontal
Superior Parietal
Descending Parietal
Inferior Parietal
Inf. Frontal
Fissure of Rolando.

It's tearing at my sanity.
My heart is pounding like a racehorse at the final stretch
Chest heavy, head too light
Room spinning like I'm on a tilt-a-whirl going way too fast.

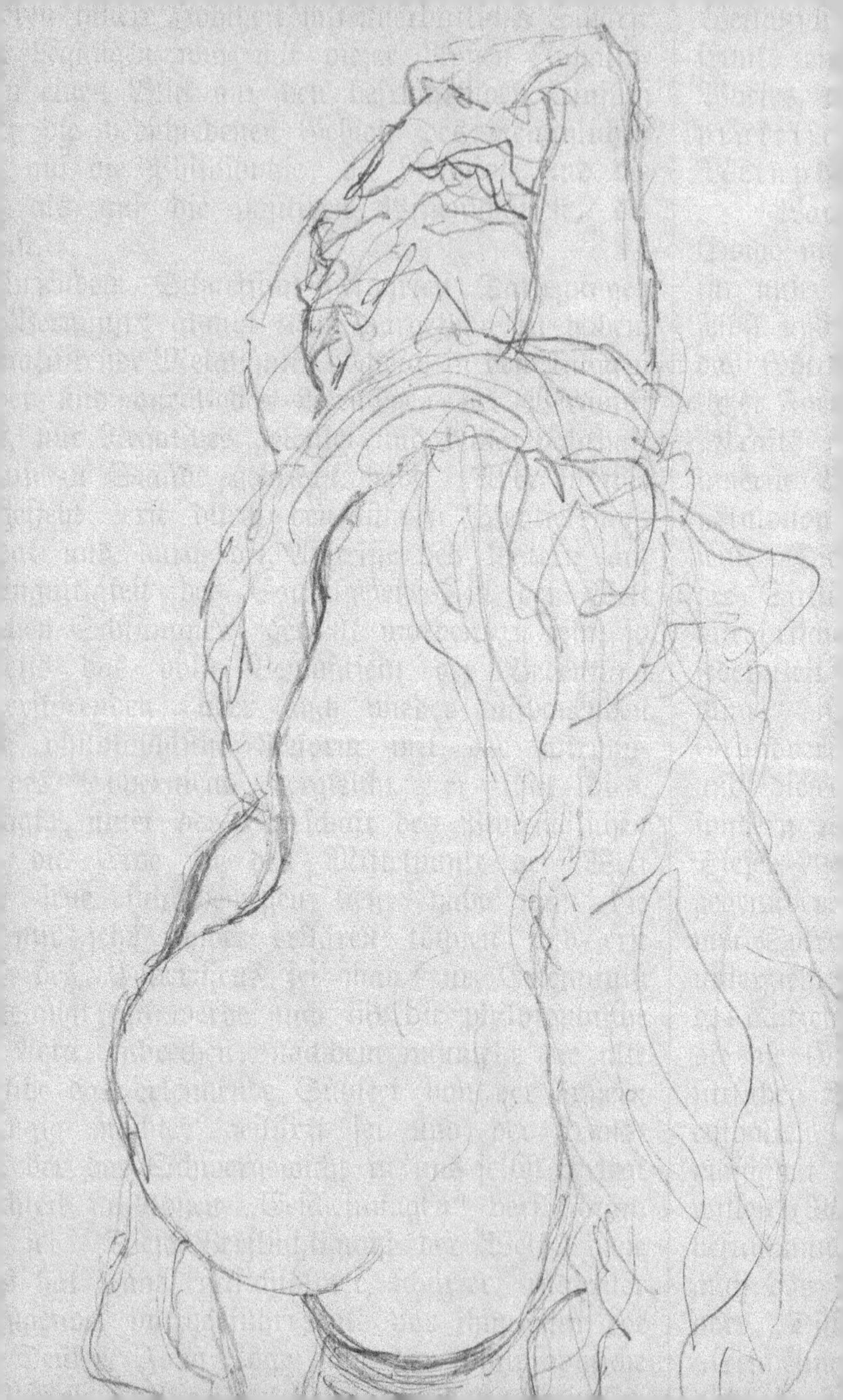

The white cotton bedsheets
Tangled with my legs
Wrapped them up
Like an unkempt necklace
Keep me drugged with sleep

The internal surface (Fig. 155) is unequally divided into two pa[rts by a hori]zontal projection of bone, the *palate process*: the portion above the

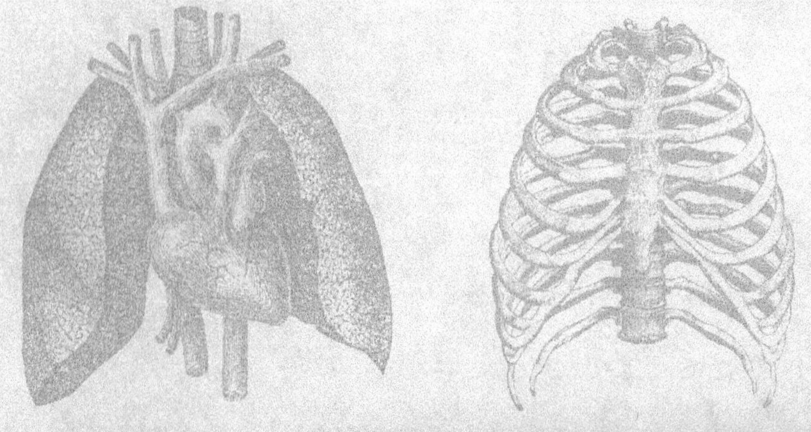

Fig. 155.—Left superior maxillary bone. Internal surface.

forms part of the outer wall of the nasal fossæ: that below it form[s] cavity of the mouth. The superior division of this surface presents a[n irregu]lar opening leading into the *antrum of Highmore*. At the upper [part of this] aperture are numerous broken cellular cavities, which in the articula[ted skull are] closed in by the ethmoid and lachrymal bones. Below the aperture

When the words come ripping you apart at 2 am
Flooding you
Demanding you breathe life onto paper
Mixing ink and blood and flesh and time
Until there is nothing left of you
Nothing but your soul dripping on the page.

Ulna.
Olecranon
Greater Sigmoid cavity
Radius.
Artic. with Humerus.
Head
Neck
FLEXOR DIGITORUM PROFUNDUS
Radial origin of FLEXOR SUBLIMIS DIGITORUM
FLEXOR LONGUS POLLICIS
PRONATOR
Styloid process
SUPINATOR LONGUS
Styloid process

As time drifts,
The lights bleed into the walls
Background noise emphasizes silence

Sisterhood.

I am part of a sisterhood. A collective of women unknown. We walk among you. We may look the same to the untrained eye, but we have lived far more than the average person.

Our lives have been full of challenges that no person should ever have to face. We look at the world, at its beauty in a different light. If you pass one of us on the street, you may never know the difference unless we allow you to. That is a gift in itself.

To know the truth, our pain, our trials, our suffering, our secret. Many hide in plain sight, some wear the sisterhood as a badge of honor, openly. It depends on their course. Many live with only a few knowing their truth, being able to count their keepers on one hand.

Mine is one of almost complete secrecy. I know only a few of the sisters because I choose to live that way, in a life of solitude, of unknown. I fight each day believing in beauty and monster within. Sometimes darkness wins and I must remind myself I am not being punished. There is a beauty and a light to all of this, that I have been given a perspective that most never fathom possible.

A life of pain and suffering may come with the sisterhood, trials of emotional and physical turmoil but they make us stronger, better human beings. Most of us have learned inner strength. We've gained the poise and grace that most Victorian-age women strived for.

Some are born with it, some receive these lessons young, and some are tried at an older age, but each learns an inner beauty and joins us in this sisterhood because they have something to offer, and we give something in return.

It's a bond forged by a similar experience, yet all of us bring a unique perspective. We fight for each other. We support one another. We may not be blood, but sisters, nonetheless.

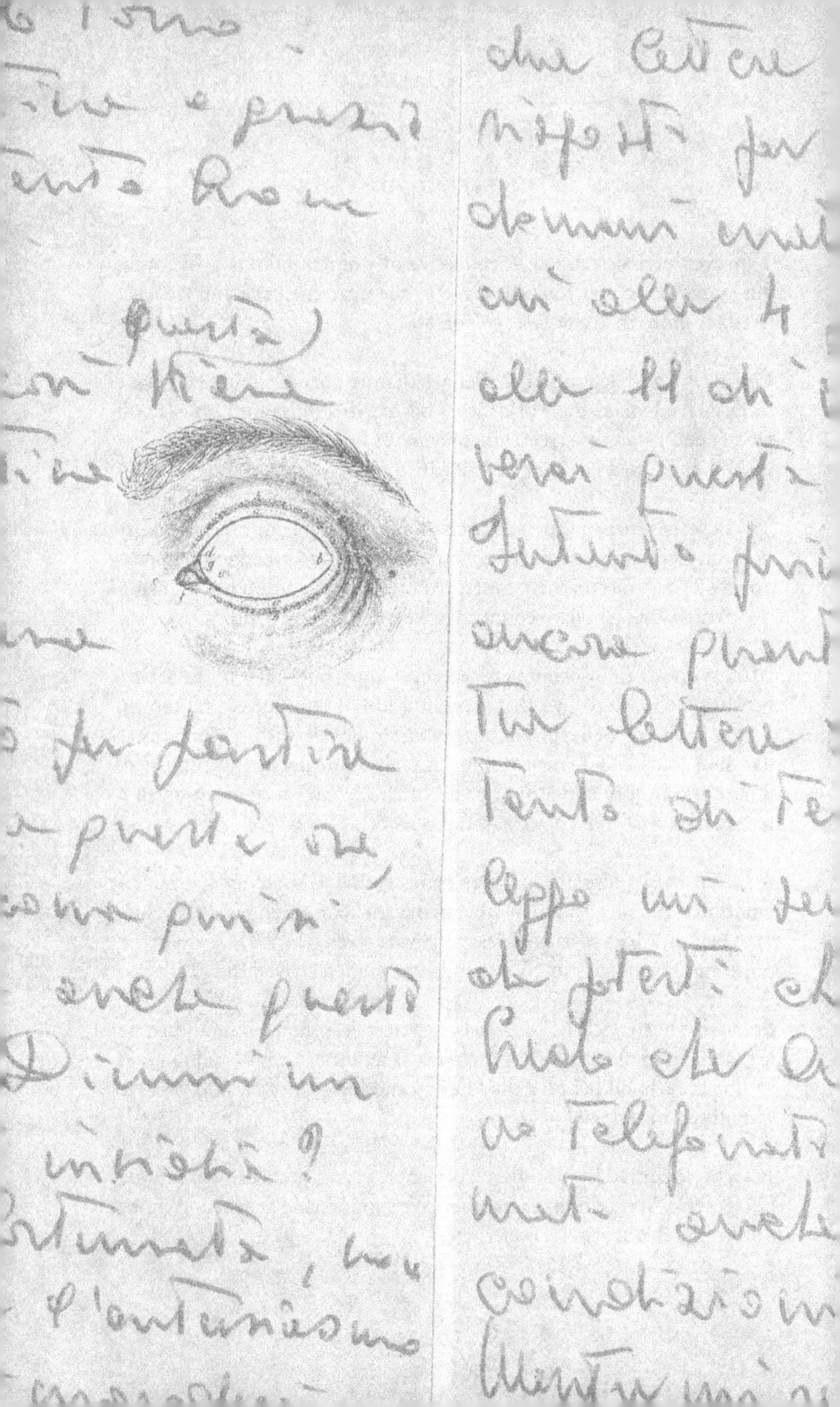

questa)
... questa ...
... per partire
... questa ...
anche questo
Dimmi un ...
... ?
... l'entusiasmo

Ashes to ashes
It's a whisper in a snowstorm
like chasing an echo
like the last flicker of light on the darkest night
it's waking up from a dream only to remember
the outline of your lover's face
Dust to Dust

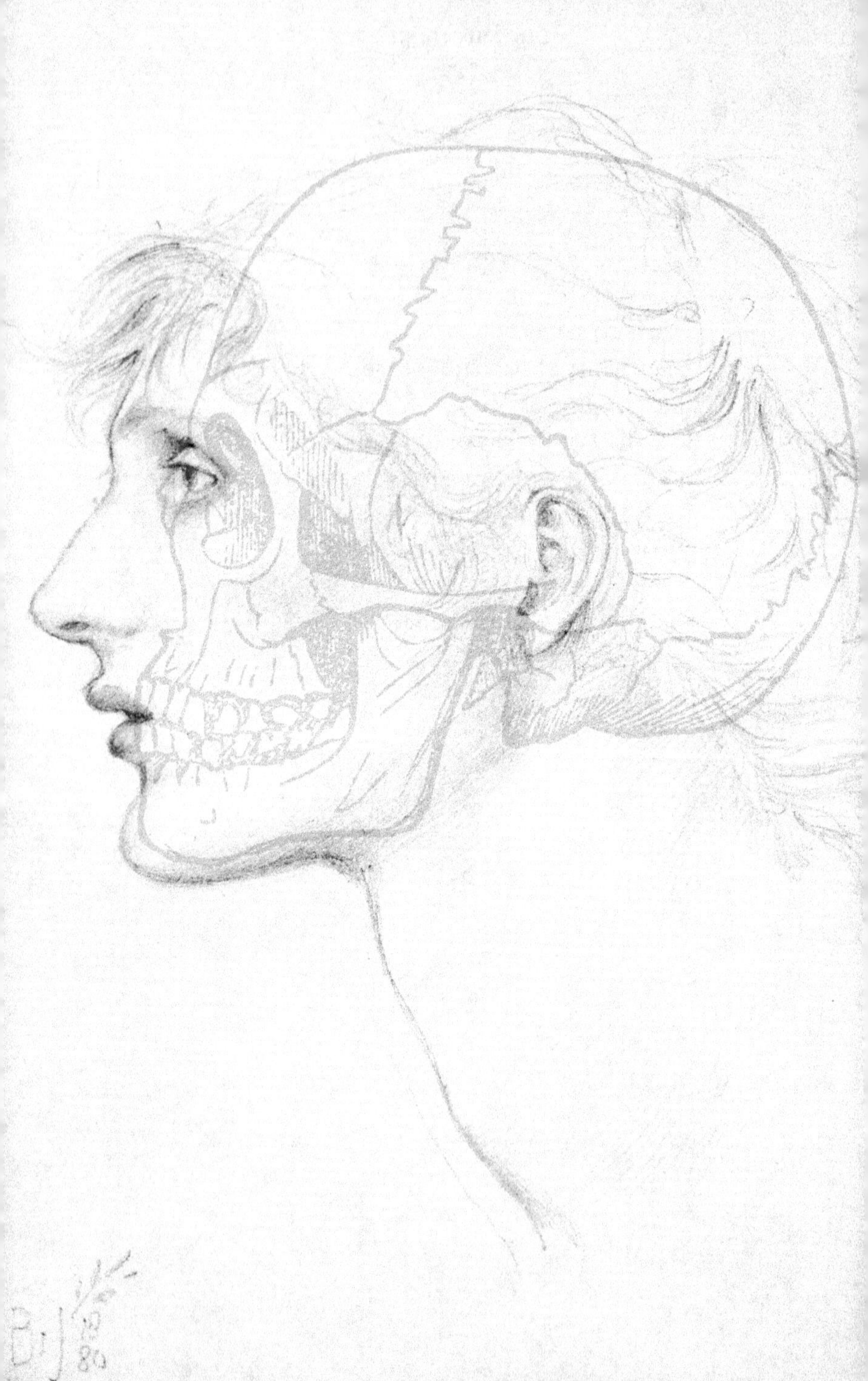

Death isn't graceful
It isn't soft or a sweet caress
It's ugly throbbing nausea
Shallow breaths that rip at your guts
It's a hollowness that swallows you
in every moment you didn't expect it

The Places of Darkness

The places of darkness are where I roam. In the depths of your deepest thoughts,
I lurk. I am in the back of your mind tearing at your sense of reality.

The burning embers were the only source of light in the cave. Her eyes hurt as they tried to adjust and failed miserably. Her pounding heart throbbed in her ears, intensifying the headache that had already begun to form. She didn't have to touch the back of her head to know there was a large bruise and blood trickling its way down her neck reminding her that she had been hit with a heavy object. She had been knocked out. She had been knocked out and kidnapped.

An unpleasant odor wafted through the cavern; the fire had been burning with something other than firewood. She just hoped that the fuel for the flames had not been another human being. She sat quietly in the deepest part of the cave where she had been dragged.

Limbs bruised and shaking, she was afraid that her night would be over in mere seconds. There were no sounds except for her heavy pants of fear. She was pressed against damp earth that seemed to soak through to her soul. She relived every moment: the camping, friends, the hiking, and going off on her own. Tears streamed down her heated face as she squeezed her eyes tighter still. She was hoping when she opened them, she would be in her room, under the covers.

She felt movement to her right, no breathing, just movement. Pain shot throughout her body, as something gripped around her neck like a vise, suffocating her slowly. She tried to squirm, make a sound, struggle, do anything! The grip only tightened more and crushed her as she moved.

A foul odor began to linger and assault her senses. Putrid, it made her eyes water, and she lost some concentration in the fight of her life. The sparse amount of light from the lost fire gave her just enough of a glimpse of her attacker's face, even if spotty from the lack of oxygen as she began to feel faint. The image made her sick as bile rose in her throat, only choking her more.

She could barely comprehend the thing as being human. His entire face was distorted, his visage deeply drawn. His skin was almost translucent and with the paleness came a mix of black, blue, and yellows. She could not see distinct features except for his mouth. That is what disturbed her, had made her accept her fate, to come to terms with her maker.

His lips were thin and chalk white, the gums a distinct blackish hue with thick saliva clinging to the discolored palate. There were attached rows of razor-sharp teeth, more like razor blades than teeth, if she had a second to reconsider. Three rows of chaotically placed shark's teeth protruding from this peaked cadaverous figure who was taking sweet pleasure in robbing her of life.

She slammed her eyes shut, accepting everything for what it was and what it had become. Envisioning her life and what would never be. She let a single word slip from her lips before the darkness overcame.

Time passed without sense, sideways twisted and intertwined. With a heavy head, she opened her crystal blue eyes and inhaled painfully. Stabbing, needle pricks engulfed every inch of her. Somehow, she had survived. She wracked her brain for what could have possibly come about to change things, to bring her back from the brink of death.

She knew it was no dream, the overwhelming pain that consumed her with each joyous breath told her that. The creature had been real. She tried to focus on those last seconds, but everything seemed to be encased in a vignette of black, trashed in slight memories of losing oxygen.

That little glimmer of light from before had long since gone out; she was in total darkness. She groped the walls, the earth crumbling and embedding itself deep into her fingernails and the cuts she had accumulated in the struggle. Every moment was an effort and felt monumental, but she pushed herself to continue to move forward. She did not know which direction she was moving, she just needed to get out. The drive was overwhelming. The time for fight had gone and flight had kicked in.

The pain in her head slashed at her focus, gnawing at her memory, reminding her of each second, she had just endured. The scent lingered, dizzying her and making her skin crawl. She shivered as if she would relive it all at any second. At the same time, she was recounting it in her brain, every second of torture tingled from the tips of her toes to her fingertips, as she slipped through the dark cave, only the fear driving her onward.

At first, she thought it was a trick of her eyes, nothing more. She did not dare to begin to hope. She was completely submerged in layers of mud, some caked on, others wet and adding weight to her body. She stopped, closed her eyes, and inhaled deeply. She was past exhausted. She knew there was still a small part of her hoping it was really light that she had just seen.

She opened her eyes again and squinted in the direction it had come from. Nothing. She pushed forward, moving millimeters. There it was again. She shifted her body and at an awkward angle, she could see a minuscule amount of light in the distance. She had somehow made it this far. She let herself crumble, to finally feel. She kept in control, but her body was wracked with tears, each droplet accompanied by shooting pain through every nerve fiber. Everything ached, burned, felt like snapping. She felt like shattering. She lay on the cool ground and counted to 100. Then slowly counted back down to one. A part of herself did not want to get up, did not want to ever move again. But she pushed herself to her knees and started crawling towards the light.

Her palms burned as they scraped against rocks; the mud on her legs shredded as it was dragged against them. She paused every few moments to wipe the hair from her face until finally she took some mud and slid it into the stray pieces to hold it back.

Finally, she reached the small hole that beamed with a halo of light above her head. Slowly, she plunged her fist through and dragged it back, grasping at the earth above. She shoved herself, squirming out of the cave, out of the horror only to hear her name being shouted in the distance, echoing off the desert rocks and bouncing back at its callers.

She heard a snap of a twig and looked up to see a familiar face walking towards her. Relief washed over her wrecked body. She lifted her hand as he reached down to her. She smiled and he smiled back. She recoiled in horror to see those same shark teeth, blackened and bloodied. He lifted her easily and plunged back into the hole. She was incapable of making a sound.

OMEGA'S DEATH
Edvard Munch, 1908-1909

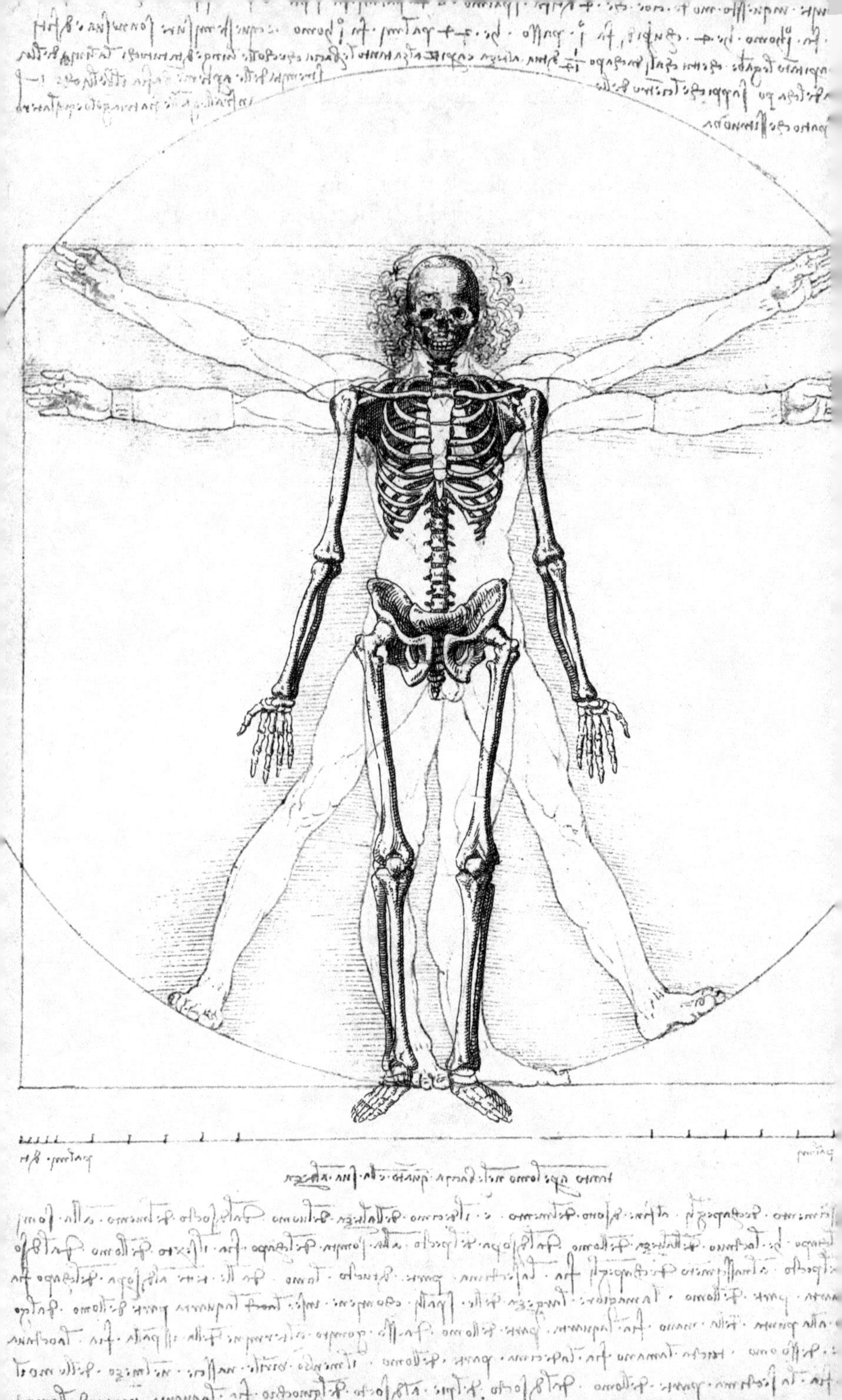

Thank you for taking the time to read this.
For giving my thoughts, poems, and stories a home.
Going through diagnosis, treatments, and loss gave life
to this book.
It was a healing experience.
It was about taking my power back.

- Kelly

Acknowledgements

I want to say thank you to my mother. She has instilled a love for the written word since I was little. To write whatever I imagined whether it be positive or negative. She always encouraged me to write it down and make stories from those feelings. She told me to follow my heart, gut, and mind. Sometimes they don't all have the same plan. She taught me that sentimentality and something heartfelt is priceless.

I want to thank my dad for a childhood filled with his voice reading me *Charlie and The Chocolate Factory* and *Chitty Chitty Bang Bang,* along with introducing me to a fantastical planet of candy and a boy named Andy. He helped fuel my imagination and creativity at a young age, and I thank him for never dimming that light.

Thank you, Matt. For always grounding me, for always reminding me the words will never dry up and that I am capable of so much even when I don't believe it. Thank you for always being a guiding light in the darkest night and reminding me that I have that light in myself as well. And finally, for teaching me I am strong even when I am fragile.

And thank you, Rachel Clift for once again helping me create another book. She knew what I had in my mind and helped create this final product. She put her time and effort into making my dreams a reality. I couldn't be more thankful she had chosen to work with me.

About the Author

Kelly Curry is an old soul based in Lake Tahoe, California where she lives with a menagerie of animals. When Kelly is not writing, she is collecting books she plans to read. This is her second collection of poetry.

THE HANDS

Edvard Munch, 1895

www.ingramcontent.com/pod-product-compliance
Lightning Source LLC
Chambersburg PA
CBHW052355060726
47592CB00020B/2363